Contemporary Latin Jazz Guitar

Volume 1

by

Neff Irizarry II

Cover Art by
Alma Linnéa Nicolasa Irizarry and Chris Volion

SHER MUSIC CO.

© 2021 Sher Music Co., P.O. Box 445, Petaluma, CA, 94953

All Rights Reserved. International Copyright Secured.

Made in the U.S.A. No part of this book may be reproduced in any form without written permission from the publisher.

ISBN – 978-0-9976617-9-8

CONTENTS

Acknowledgments 1

Introduction 3
   How to Use This Book 4
   Recommended Fingerings and Positions 4
   Helpful Tips 9

Chapter 1: *Clave*, *Cáscara*, and *Tumbao* 10
   Clave 10
   Cáscara 26
   Tumbao 49

Chapter 2: *Guajeos* and *Montunos* 58
   Guajeo and *Montuno* Comparison Chart 85
   Tres, *Cuatro* and *Requinto* Adaptations to the Guitar 86
   Piano Adaptations and Solutions for the Guitar 102
   How to Interact with the Pianist 108

Chapter 3: Left & Right Hand Technique for *Guajeos/Montunos* 117

Chapter 4: Traditional Styles 120

Chapter 5: Influential Guitarists 129
   Juanito "El Maestro" Márquez 130
   Paul "Payo" Alicea 130
   Sonny Henry 131
   Edgardo Miranda 131
   Carlos Emilio "El Gordo" Morales 132
   Bobby Redfield 133
   Carlos Santana 135
   Steve Khan 135

Chapter 6: Latin Jazz and the Jazz Guitarist 137

Chapter 7: Improvisation, Transcription and Analysis 155

Chapter 8: Compositions and Play-Along Tracks. 168

    Play-Along Compositions 177

Play-Along Track List. 184

Anthology of Influential Guitarists in Latin Jazz 191

Timeline of Selected Recordings 192

Credits 195

About the Author 197

ACKNOWLEDGMENTS

To Steve Khan for investing so much of yourself in me both personally and professionally.

To Victor Mendoza for always fostering and challenging my abilities as an academic and performer.

To Antonio Mendoza for sharing your penultimate guitar memoirs with me.

To Arturo O'Farrill, Brent Fischer, Bobby Sanabria and Richie Zellon for graciously granting me interviews.

To Curt Mangan Strings, Vovox Cables, Reflector Audio USA, and Scharpach Guitars for their support.

To the Pittsburgh Foundation Paul J Baum Scholarship for generously supporting my Master's Thesis, which led to this publication.

To Taiteen Edistämiskeskus-Taike for generously supporting this book.

To Leslie López and Ricardo Padilla for your friendship and performances.

To Tomás "Matanzas" Jimeno for your support.

To Jimmy Haslip for your unending support.

To my two daughters, Lilja Solveig and Alma Linnéa Nicolasa Irizarry.

To my dearest wife, Liga Sakne, for your unending support and patience during this time.

*This is book is dedicated to my mother,
Georgina Lozada Irizarry*

INTRODUCTION

If you are reading this book, then you came for definitive answers on how to incorporate the guitar into contemporary Latin jazz. The solutions that I offer within this text are new readaptations of the precedents played by folkloric instruments and what legendary guitarists and bandleaders have already developed. However, I also add a new perspective that makes use of the guitar's sonority, technical qualities, and similarities with well-known jazz guitar voicing techniques. This, in turn, will get you straight to the point of making Latin music and keeping up with those pianists!

In today's definition of the word, "Latin jazz" is very ambiguous because it encompasses not only the Afro-Antillean influence but the Central American, South American, and Brazilian influence. Everything from bossa nova to *cumbia* to *son* to flamenco to tango mixed with jazz might be considered as Latin jazz. However, Latin jazz is originally the music derived from Cubop and that unique development created by musicians in New York City. Therefore, my primary focus is on the Afro-Cuban variety of Latin jazz and how the electric guitar's role evolved within the style.

To many, the achievements of Carlos Santana established the guitar's role in Latin Music. Carlos blended mainstream blues-rock, over-driven guitar sounds with Latin rhythms. However, even though his achievements did put the electric guitar on the Latin music map, other guitarists of equal importance helped lay the necessary groundwork to establish its role within the Latin jazz genre.

The adaptation and development of the electric guitar's role in Latin jazz from its traditional beginnings in Latin music are truly undocumented or rarely mentioned. Valuable recordings that display how the guitar forged its voice in Latin jazz are scarce to come by. However, we wouldn't have had the possibility nor the conditions to create a space for modern guitarists if it wasn't for these earlier guitarists who paved the way.

INTRODUCTION

Contemporary Latin Jazz Guitar will look at some of those guitarists and their vanguard techniques that forged and defined Latin jazz guitar.

With the information compiled here, I have created a step-by-step approach based upon clear and realistic examples that will help you to understand and execute the role of the guitar in Latin jazz.

Among other goals, one objective of this book is to present a method for the guitarist to play logical readaptations of the *tres*, *cuatro*, *requinto* and piano in a Latin jazz format.

How to Use This Book

Each chapter will focus on a particular subject followed by exercises developed for the guitar that help to practice the concept. After the exercises, a brief paragraph is added to help you analyze your performance. Keep a journal, be creative, listen to the examples, check out the selected discography section and play along with your favorite recordings.

Recommended Fingerings and Positions

There are many schools of thought on fingerings and positions. Therefore, I encourage you to find your own fingerings and positions that enable you to enjoy the exercises according to your own technical facility.

However, my criteria for fingerings and positions are the following:

1. Sound and timbre.

2. Derived from triads and intervallic structures.

3. Ergonomic.

4. Horizontal and vertical placement that enables ease of movement to the next phrase.

So, in the hopes of improving the learning process, I have included a few examples with standard tablature notation so that you can get an idea about how I would play these exercises.

INTRODUCTION

These fingerings and inferred position choices are supported by the *Guajeo/Montuno* Chart on page 85 and Chapter 3. Please apply the same fingering choices and variations to the other exercises throughout the book.

For more detailed information, please visit my website where I will include short video demonstrations of each exercise.

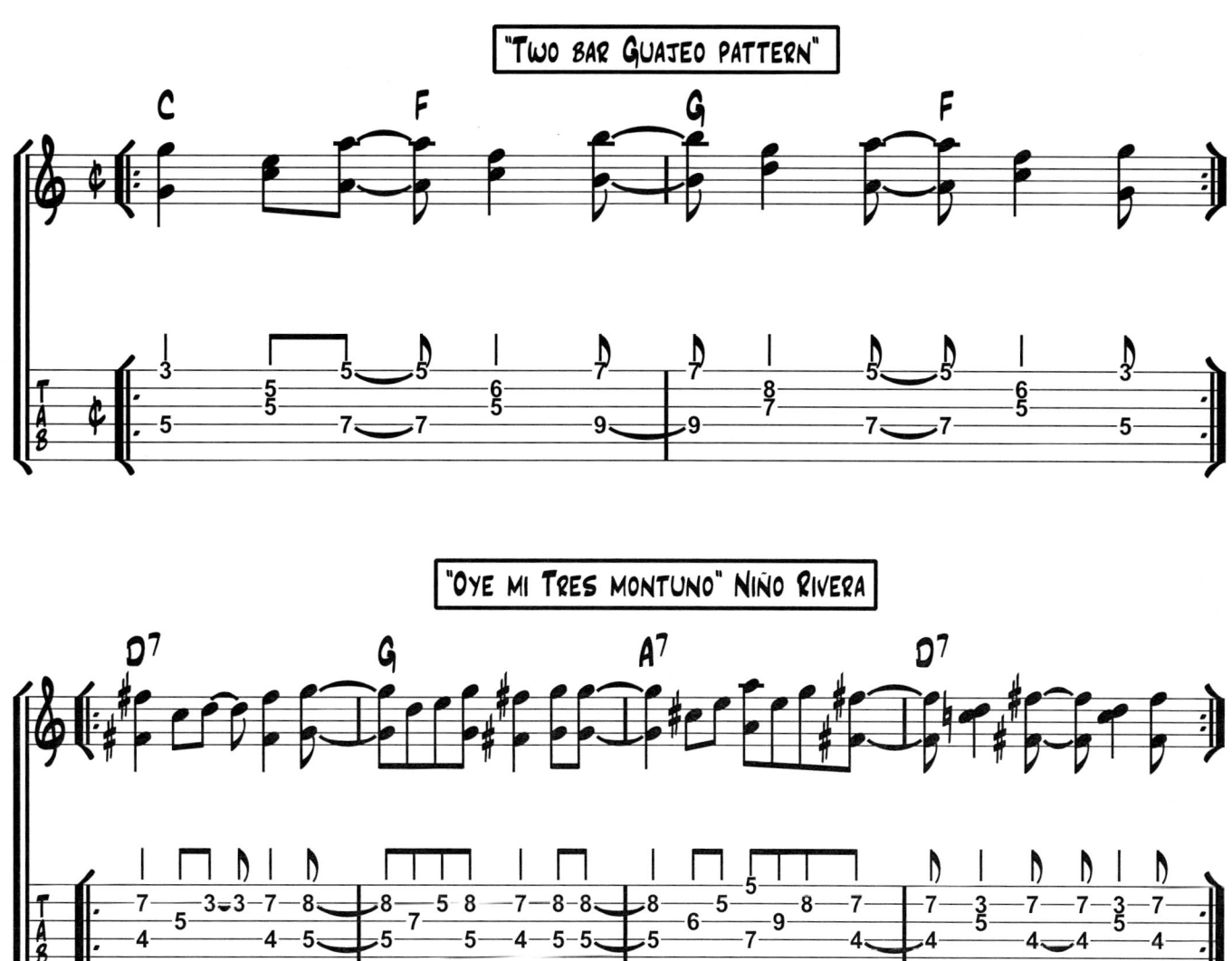

INTRODUCTION

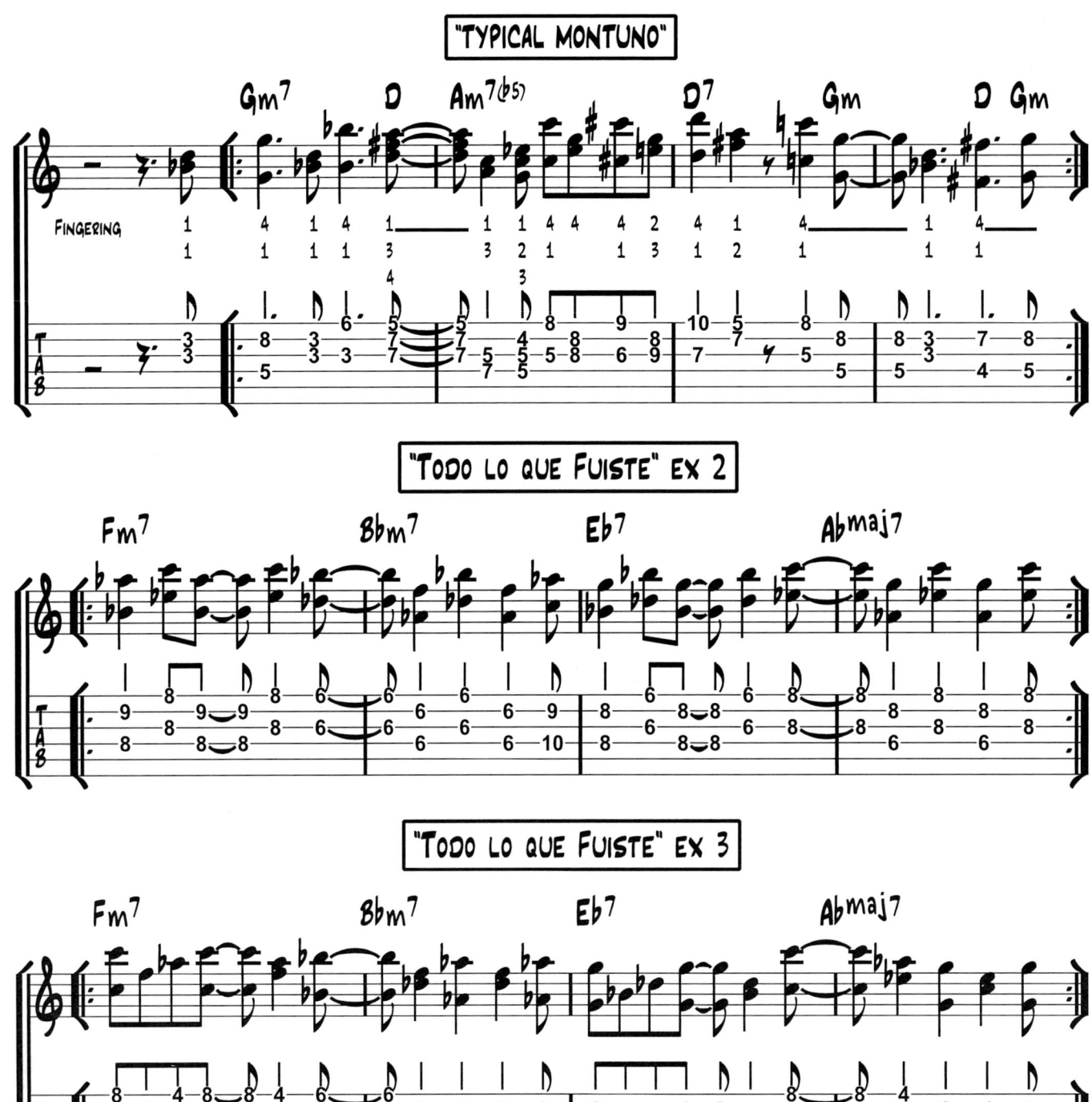

INTRODUCTION

"Guajeo/Montuno"

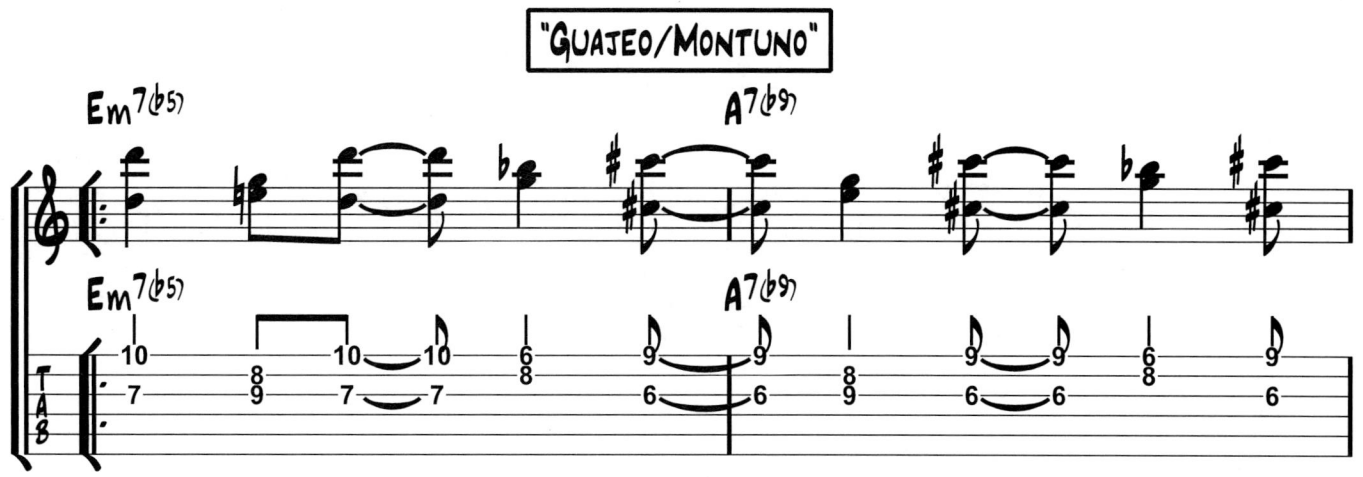

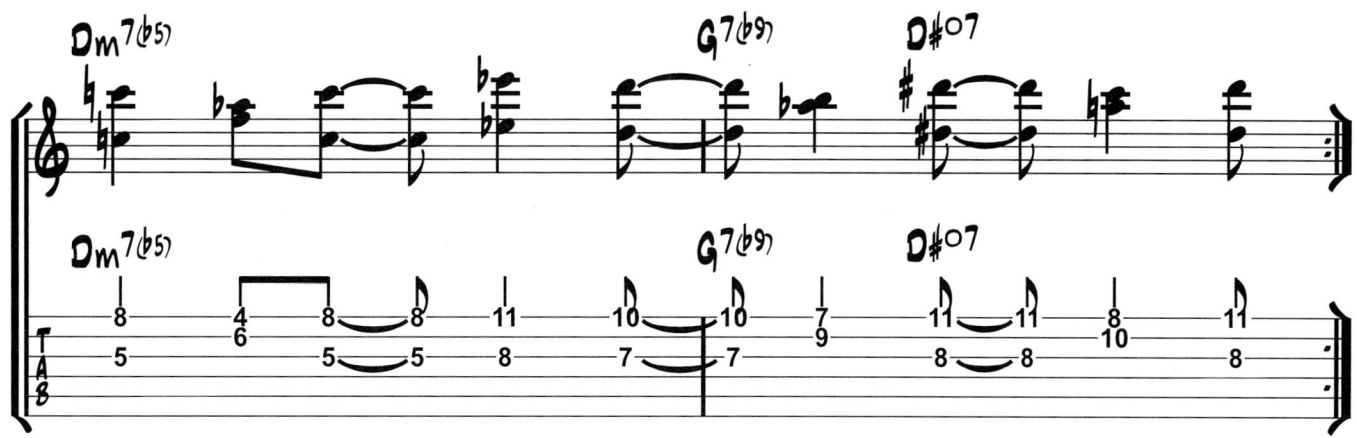

INTRODUCTION

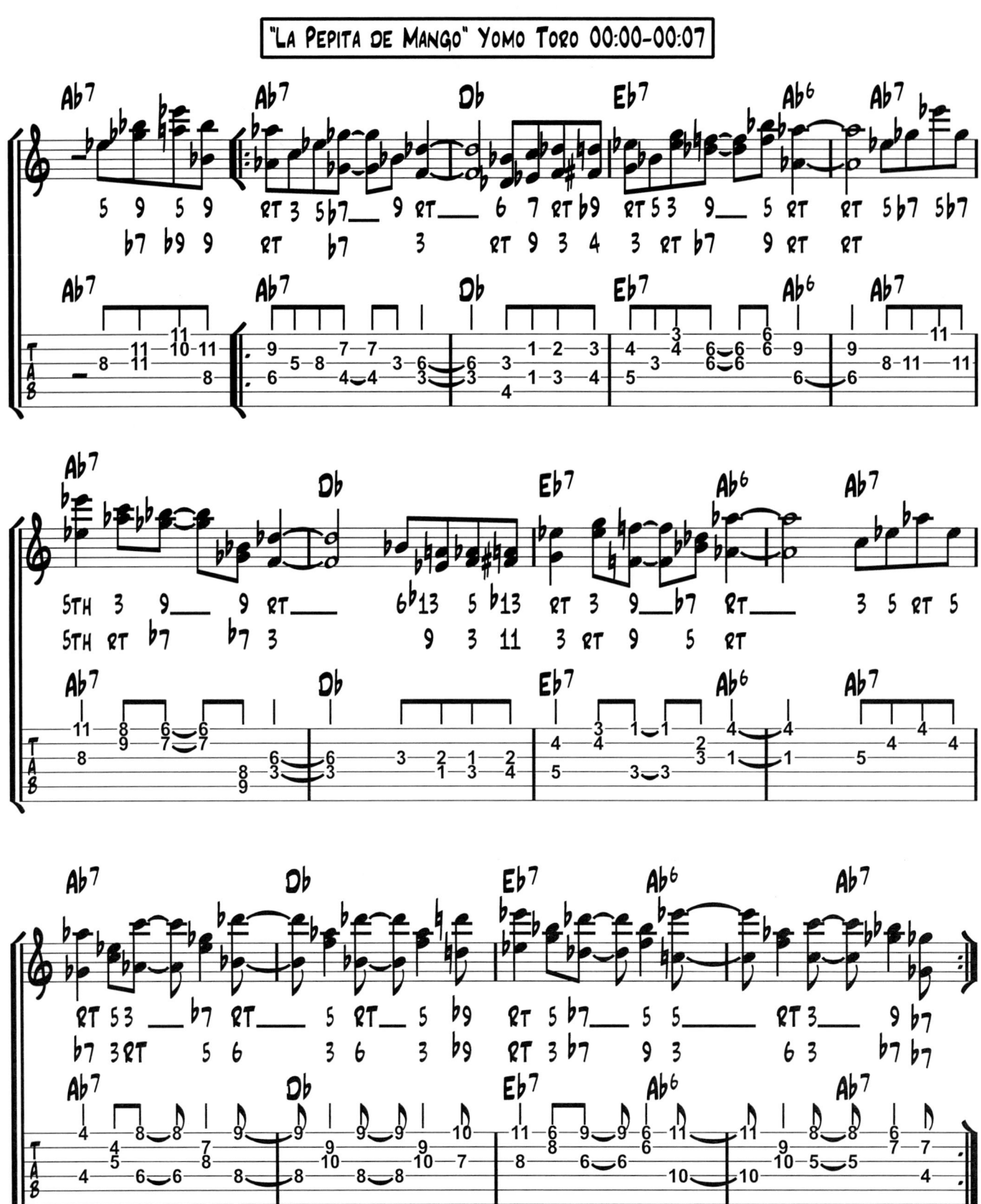

INTRODUCTION

Helpful Tips

1. Use a metronome and subdivide.

2. Isolate passages.

3. Analyze exercises.

4. Compare articulations with the recordings.

5. When listening to the discography, ask yourself which *guajeo* or *montuno* technique does one use during each part of the song?

The amazing techniques pioneered by Latin jazz guitarists are made of creative ideas that others dared to think possible. However, so can you! ¡¡*Suerte!!*

For all artist transcription and audio example links, visit:

https://neffirizarry.com/resources/

Please feel free to contact me at

https://www.neffirizarry.com

for bookings, clinics, lectures, master classes and private lessons.

CHAPTER 1

Clave, Cáscara, and *Tumbao*

In order to play Latin jazz with stylistic integrity, the guitarist must be familiar with the most fundamental rules of Afro-Cuban music. These rules are about *clave, cáscara* and *tumbao* rhythmic patterns. Each section of this chapter will define the basic pattern and offer ways to incorporate them in your playing. Then, the subsequent chapters will show how they relate to the *guajeos, montunos* and *tumbaos* that allow the guitar to thrive in this rich musical heritage.

It is important to note that there are many different variations of the basic *cáscara* and *tumbao* patterns. Therefore, it is suggested that you consult other reference books and recordings that focus on those areas in question.

Clave

All Afro-Cuban music adheres to some type of an ostinato key rhythm called *clave*. "*Clave*: A five-note, bi-measure pattern which serves as the foundation for all of the rhythmic styles in salsa music. The *clave* consists of a 'strong' measure containing three notes (also called the *tresillo*), and a 'weak' measure containing two notes, resulting in patterns beginning with either measure, referred to as 'three-two' or 'two-three.' The *clave* is the first fundamental rhythmic pattern that connects all other Afro-Cuban rhythms together. There are two types of *clave* patterns associated with popular (secular) music: *son clave* and *rumba clave*."[1]

---

[1] *101 Montunos* by Rebeca Mauleón (Sher Music Co., Petaluma, CA, 1999).

CHAPTER 1 — CLAVE, CÁSCARA, AND TUMBAO

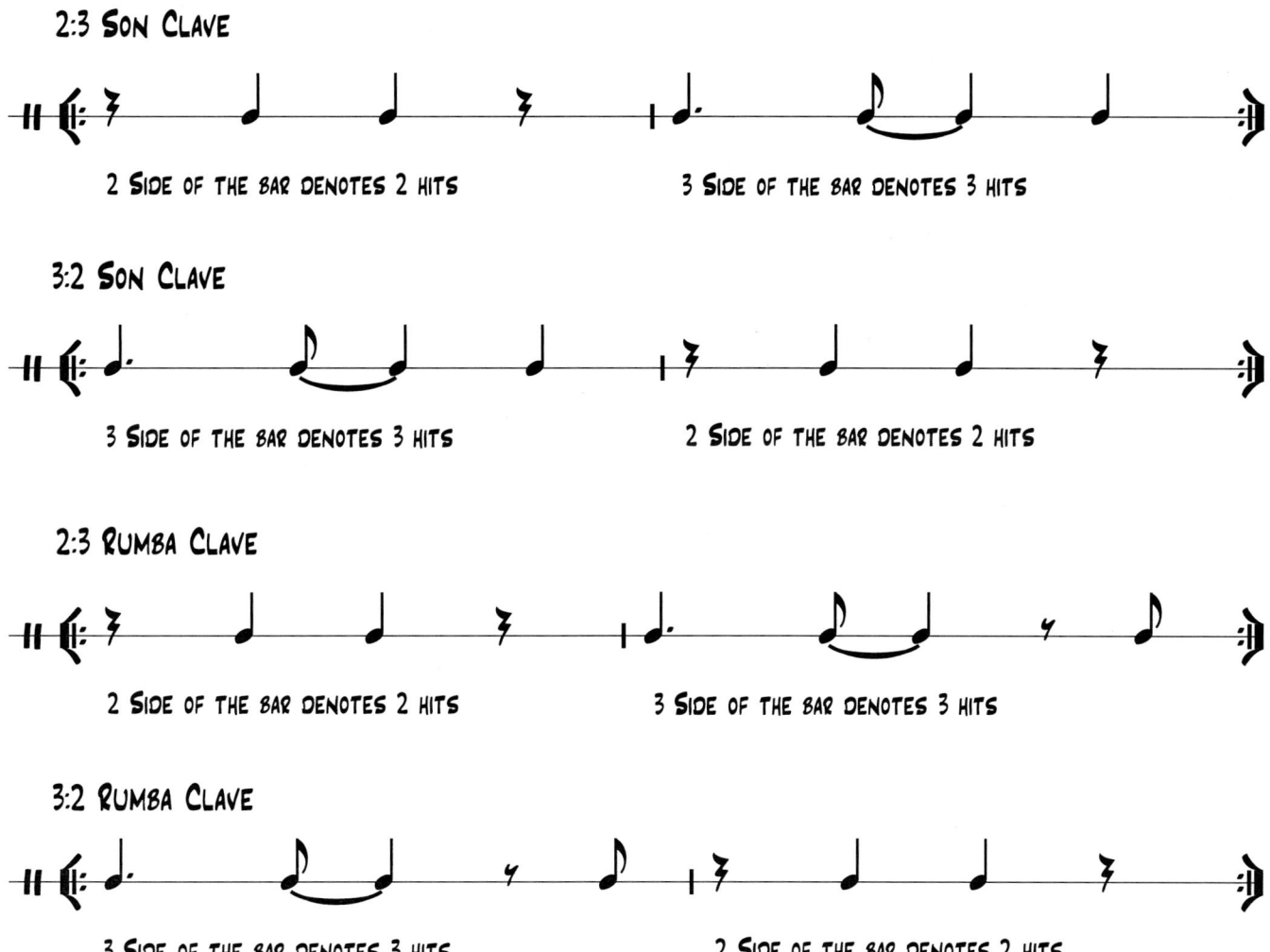

One of the most challenging things about playing the *clave* is to play it consistently in time at various tempi. You might want to try to subdivide eighth notes while you play or even use the *cáscara* pattern in the next section so that you may ensure an accurate and stable time feel.

In order to get accustomed to playing the *clave*, we will now review rhythmic subdivisions and adapt well-known chord progressions to the *clave* pattern. However, this is only for practice and is not intended as a rhythmic pattern to be played consistently in a performance situation. The Latin jazz guitarist would never play the exact *clave* pattern in a playing situation, except occasionally in unison with the band at the end of a section or in a break.

As you will see later, these practice etudes will help to plant the rhythm in your soul so that you can slowly understand how to embellish it.

CHAPTER 1 — CLAVE, CÁSCARA, AND TUMBAO

Recommended Mode of Practice

1. Feeling the subdivision. **Play-Along Tracks 1-7**

It is extremely important for you to feel the subdivision in order to play in a consistent time feel. The very nature of playing and understanding syncopated rhythms depends on feeling the subdivision.

In the following examples, I have written a steady eighth-note pattern with accents over the eighth notes that line up with the *clave*. By practicing these exercises from slow to fast, you will begin to feel the *clave* and be able to play it in time, consistently.

CHAPTER 1   CLAVE, CÁSCARA, AND TUMBAO

2. *Clave* on for one bar and then off for the next bar. **Play-Along Tracks 9-15**

Once you have practiced the subdivision exercise, we can begin to practice playing with one bar of the *clave* and then playing the missing side of the *clave* in both *son* and *rumba clave*.

In the first bar of the 2:3 *son clave* example, you will play the 2-side of the *clave* rhythm. However, in the second bar, it's your turn to play the 3-side of the *clave* in the silence. Remember to actively use the subdivision technique from the previous example. Later on, you can think about the *cáscara* pattern or even the *tumbao* to enable a consistent time feel.

CHAPTER 1 — CLAVE, CÁSCARA, AND TUMBAO

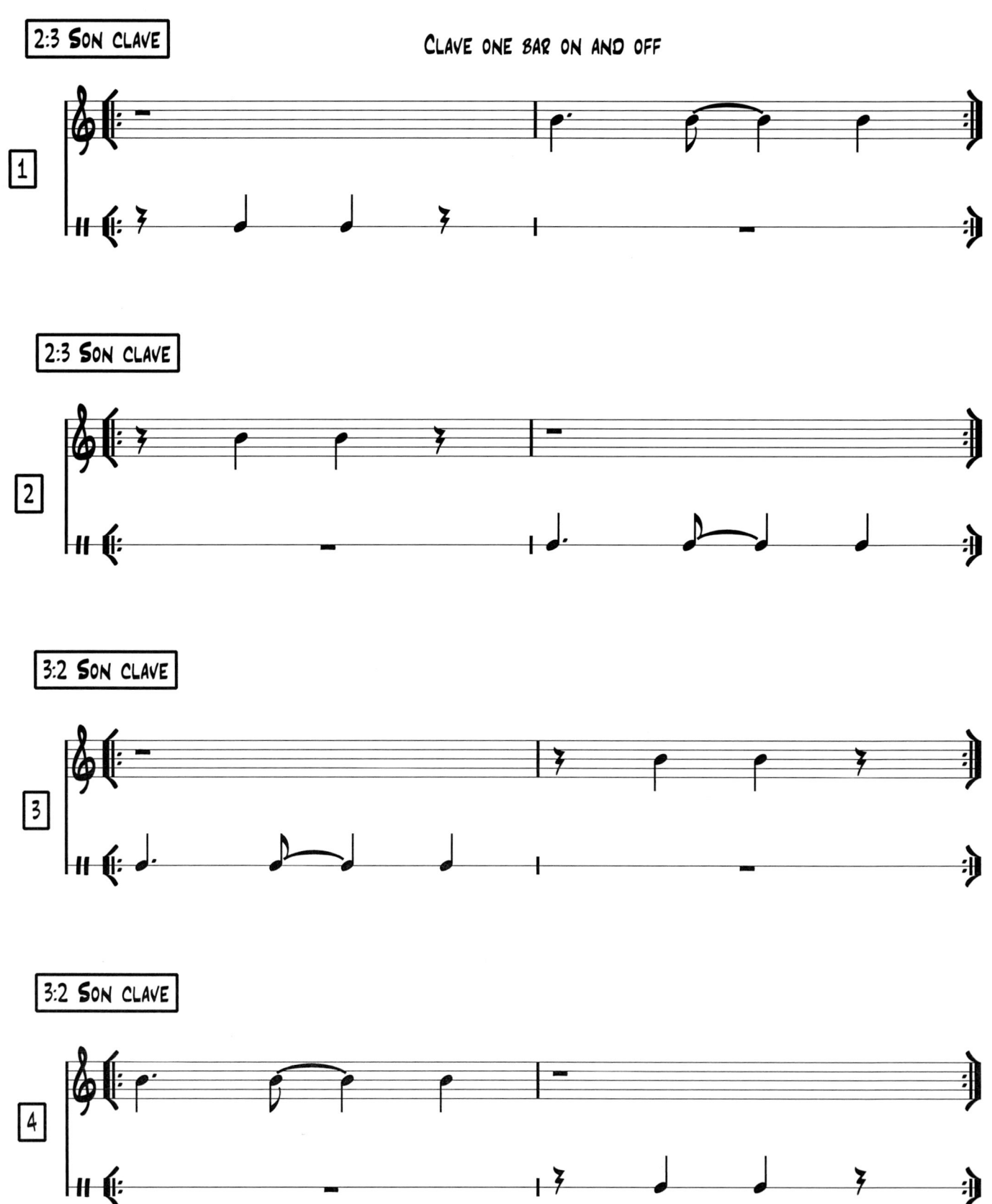

CHAPTER 1

CLAVE, CÁSCARA, AND TUMBAO

Play-Along Tracks 17-23

CHAPTER 1   *CLAVE, CÁSCARA, AND TUMBAO*

3. Chords in *Clave*. **Play-Along Tracks 25-31**

In the next exercises we will accent the *clave* pattern using familiar chord progressions. Once you have practiced all of these, concentrate on making your own variations based upon the advanced approach. Have fun!

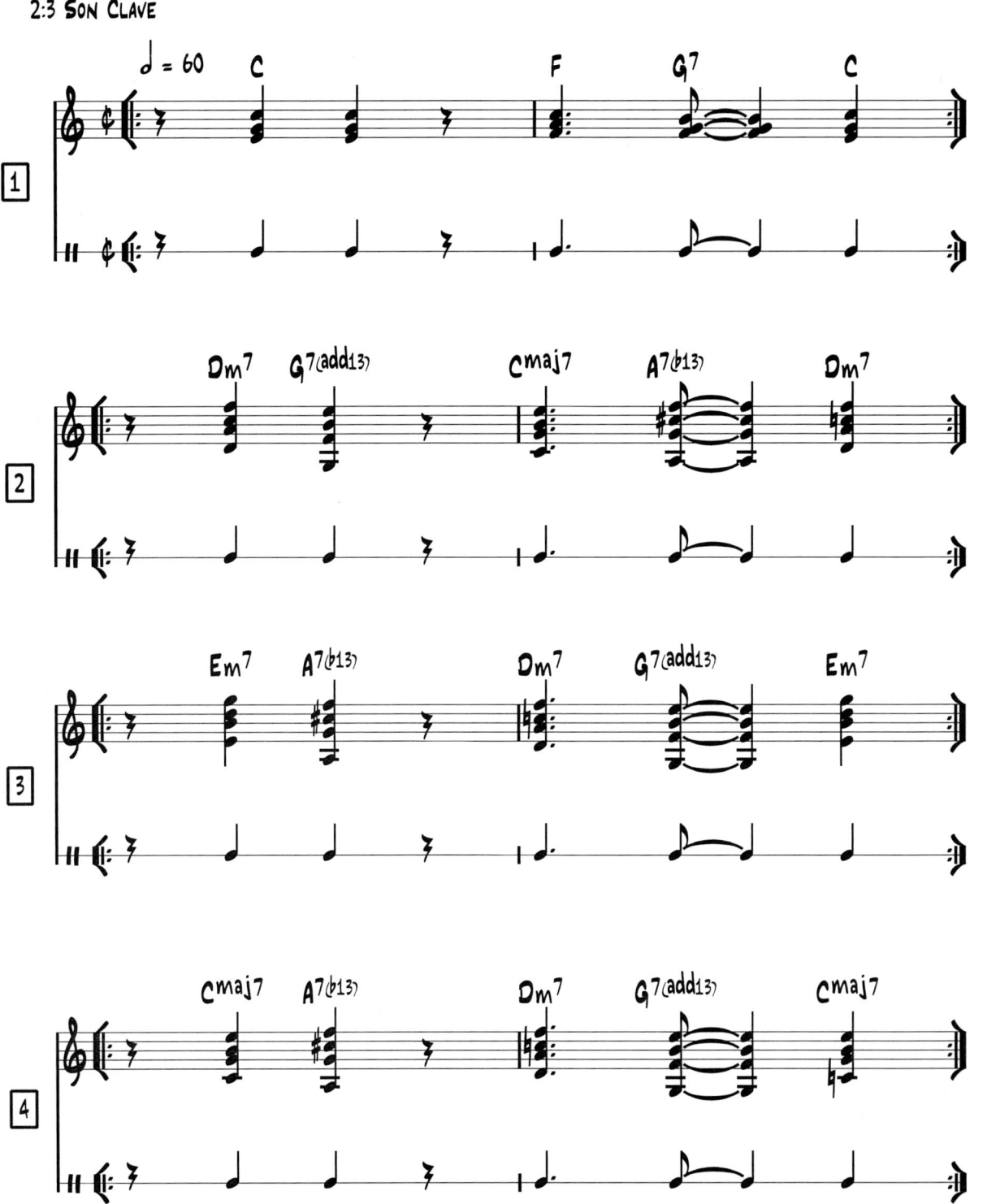

CHAPTER 1

CLAVE, CÁSCARA, AND TUMBAO

Play-Along Tracks 33-39

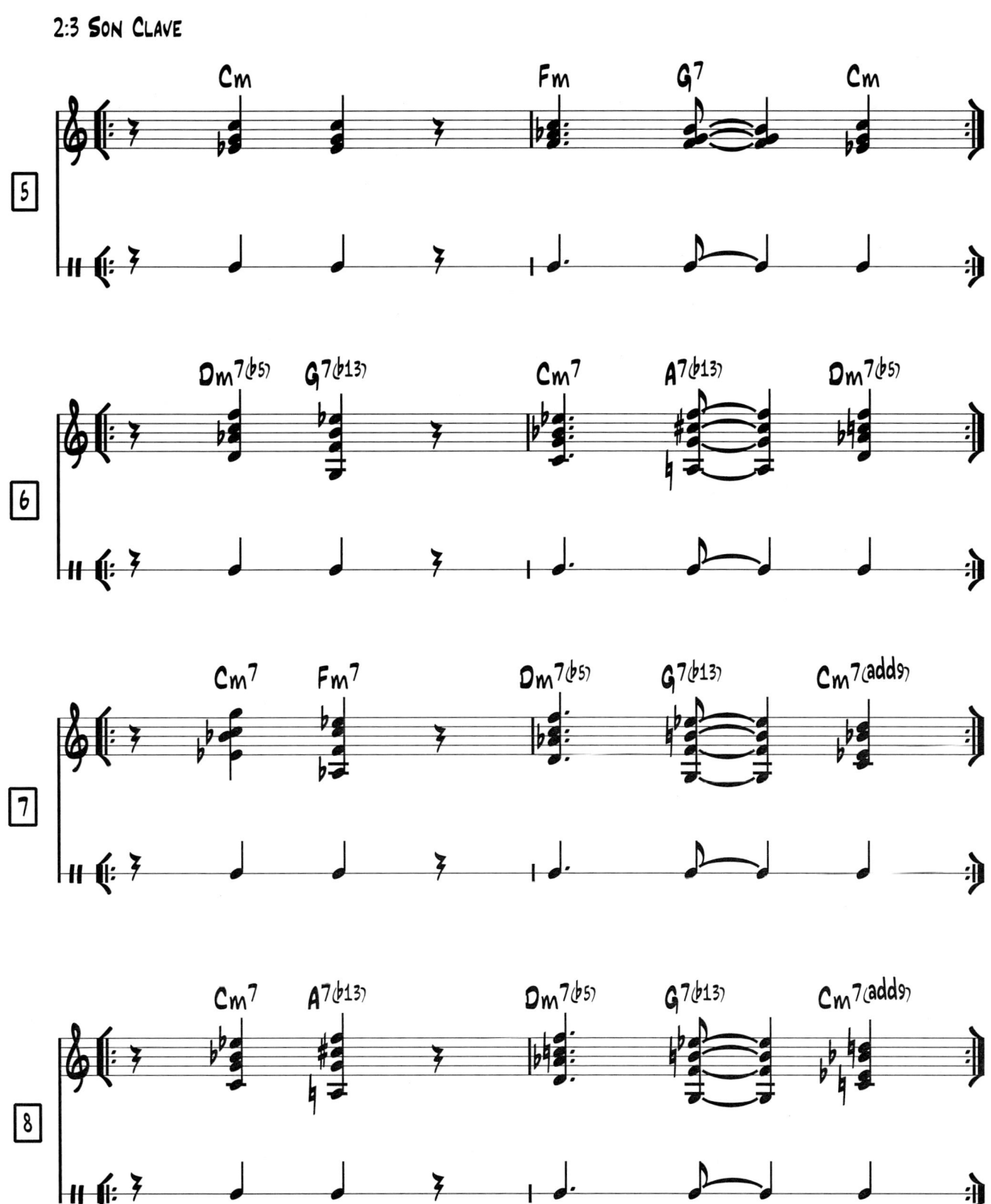

CHAPTER 1

CLAVE, CÁSCARA, AND TUMBAO

Play-Along Tracks 41-47

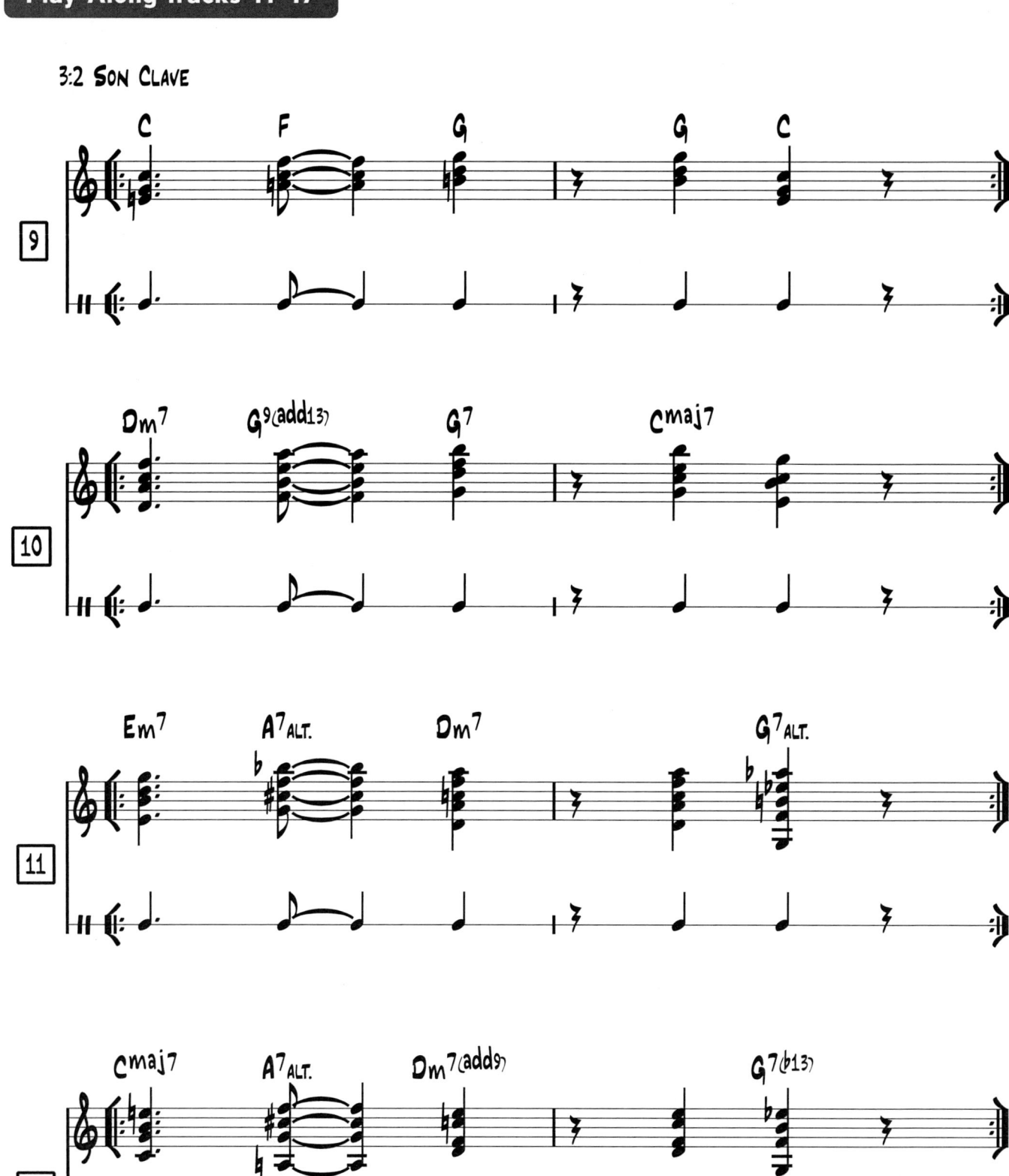

CHAPTER 1

CLAVE, CÁSCARA, AND TUMBAO

Play-Along Tracks 49-55

3:2 Son Clave

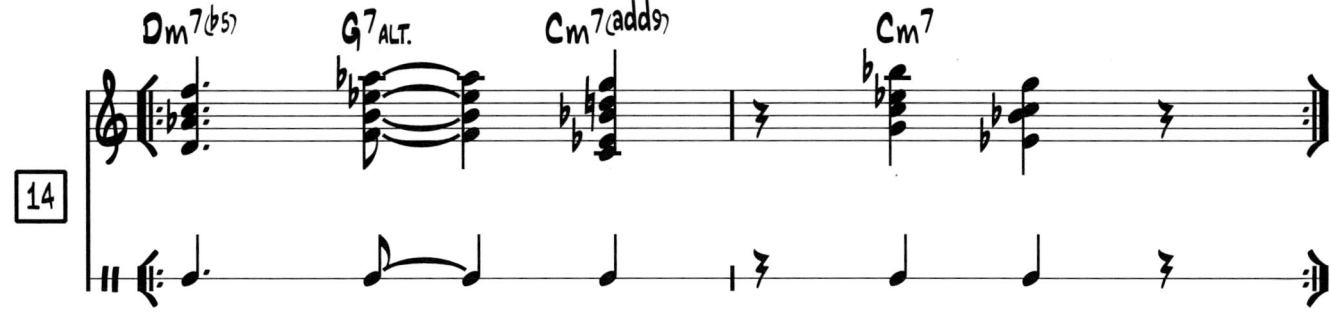

CHAPTER 1

CLAVE, CÁSCARA, AND *TUMBAO*

Play-Along Tracks 57-63

2:3 Rumba Clave

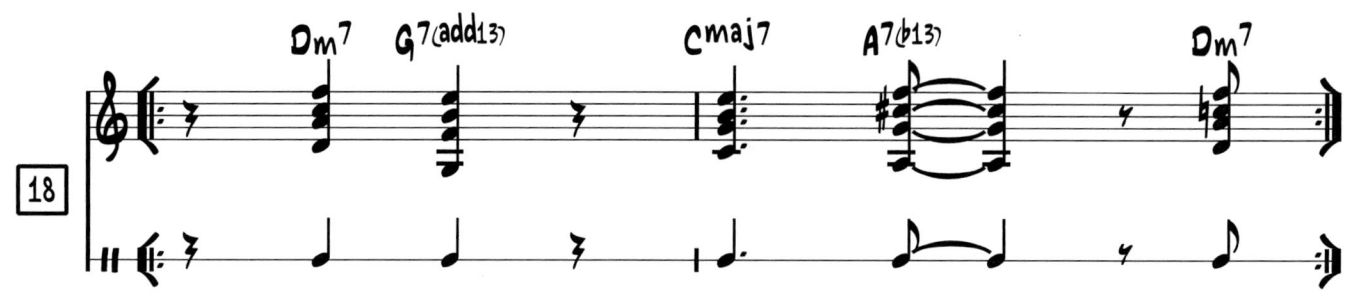

CHAPTER 1

CLAVE, CÁSCARA, AND TUMBAO

Play-Along Tracks 65-71

2:3 Rumba Clave

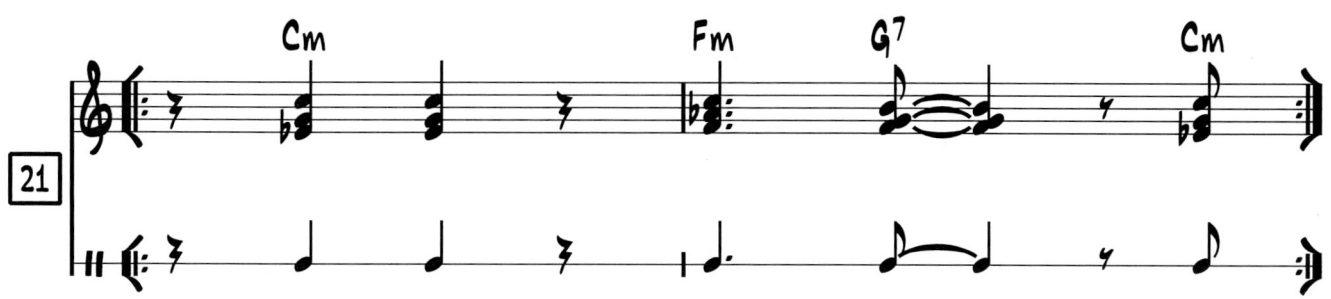

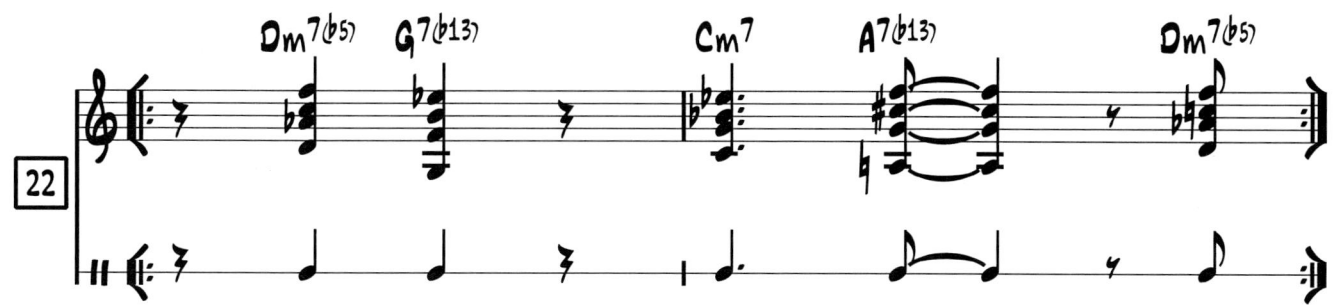

CHAPTER 1

CLAVE, CÁSCARA, AND TUMBAO

Play-Along Tracks 73-79

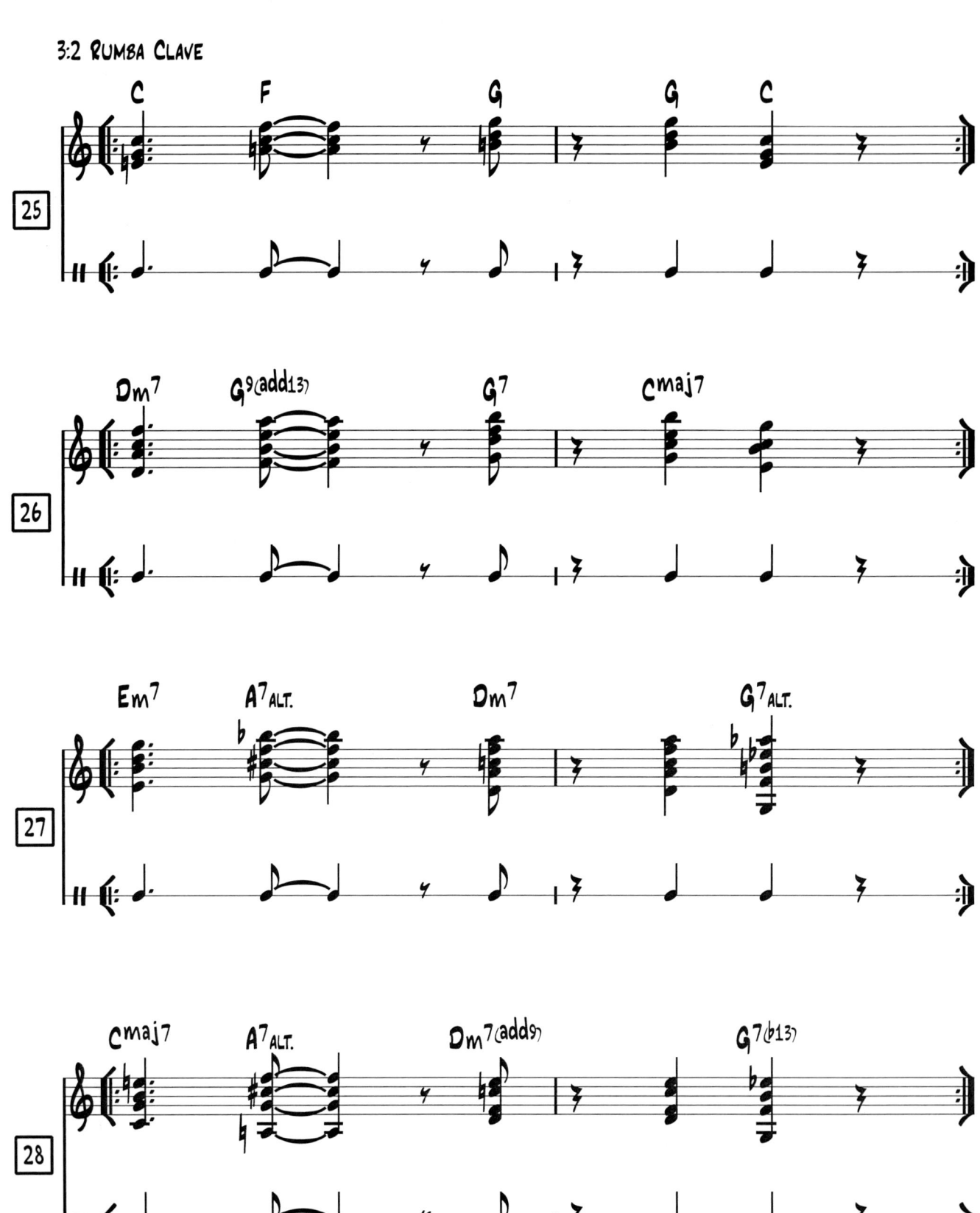

CHAPTER 1   *CLAVE, CÁSCARA,* AND *TUMBAO*

Play-Along Tracks 81-87

CONTEMPORARY LATIN JAZZ GUITAR, VOL. 1

CHAPTER 1   CLAVE, CÁSCARA, AND TUMBAO

For inspiration, here's an example from the iconic recording of "Old Devil Moon" by Benson & Farrell. Notice, as shown by the vertical lines, how George Benson accents the *clave* rhythm on the down beat of the two-side, and on the upbeat and downbeat on the three-side of the *clave*.

George Benson Comping in *Clave*

In the following four-bar examples, I have accentuated the beats where the *clave* has been accented. Notice that we are holding or sustaining the chord over the bar line while accenting the next available pulse that rhythmically aligns with the *clave*. This advanced concept is widely used by many players in Latin jazz. This is a way of creating rhythmic tension and release while implying the *clave*.

The following etudes show an advanced approach of how to imply the *clave* rhythm without accenting each pulse of the *clave*.

CHAPTER 1 — CLAVE, CÁSCARA, AND TUMBAO

Play-Along Tracks 89-95

2:3 Son Clave

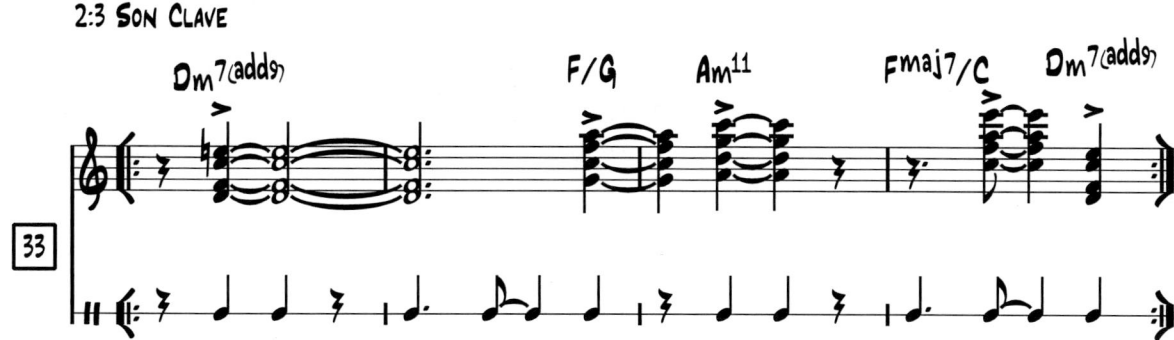

3:2 Son Clave

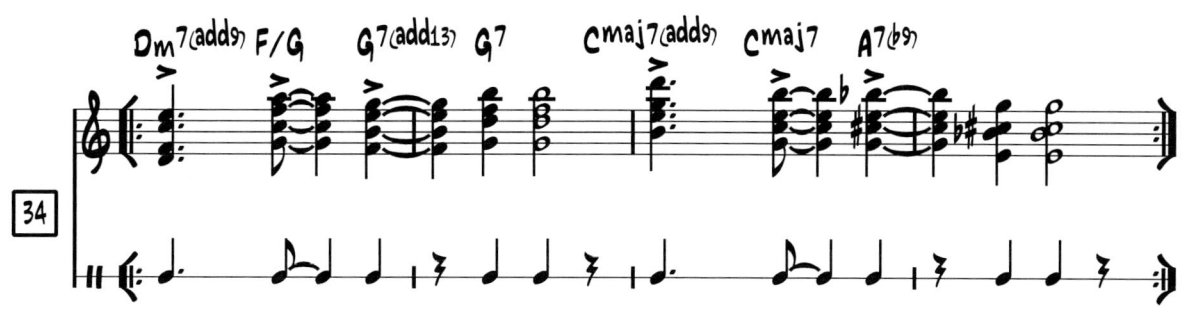

2:3 Rumba Clave

3:2 Rumba Clave

CONTEMPORARY LATIN JAZZ GUITAR, VOL. 1

Cáscara

Accompanying the *clave*, we have an ostinato pattern called "*cáscara.*" The word *cáscara* literally means "shell," and refers to the shell or sides of the drum. The *cáscara* is also the rhythmic pattern which is played on the sides of the timbales; it is a two-measure phrase, and fits with the *clave*.[2] Notice how and where the *cáscara* and the *clave* align on the downbeat and the upbeat.

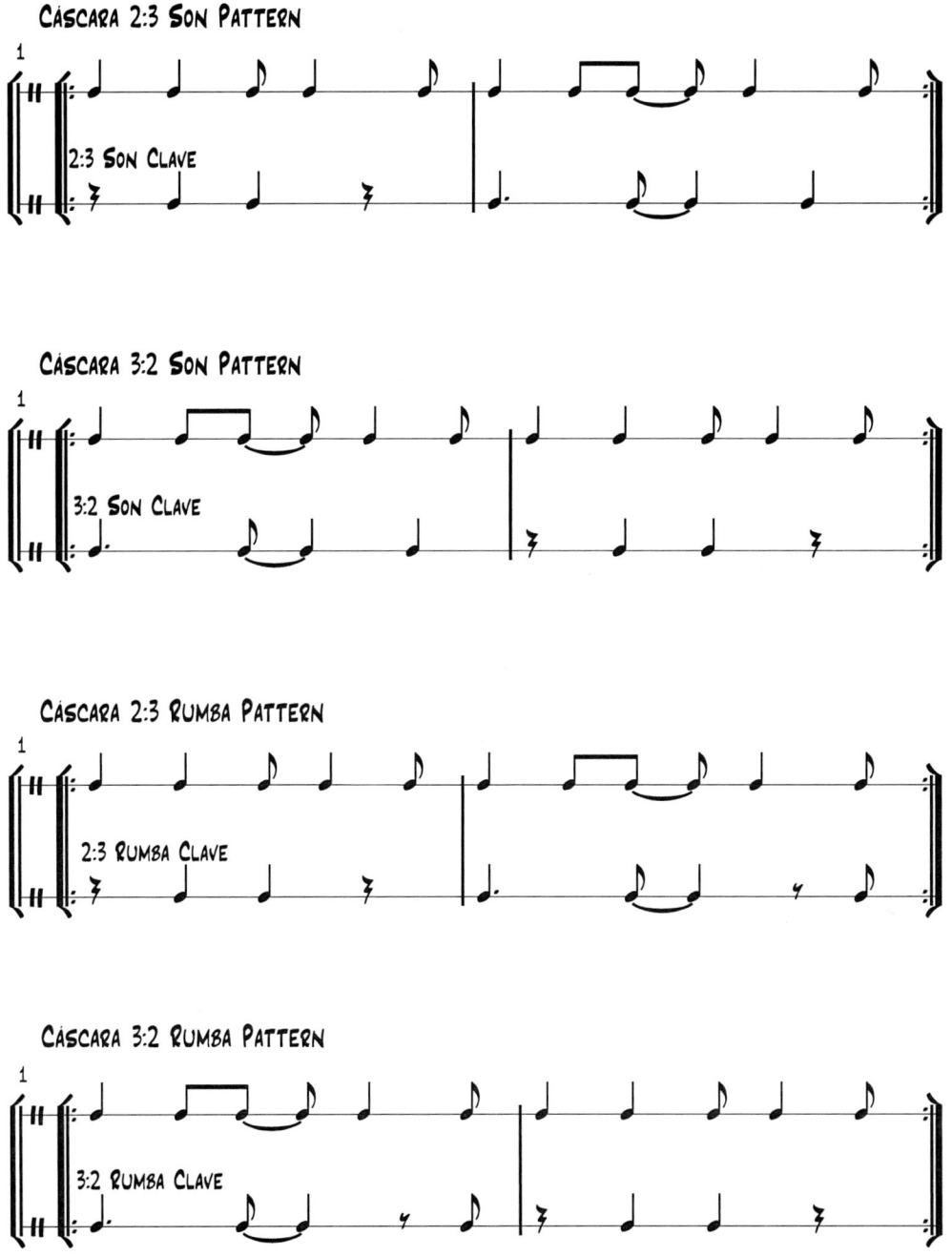

---

2   Rebeca Mauleón, *Salsa Guidebook for Piano and Ensemble* (Petaluma, CA: Sher Music, 1993).

CHAPTER 1

CLAVE, CÁSCARA, AND TUMBAO

In order to get accustomed to playing the *cáscara*, we will now review rhythmic subdivisions and then adapt well-known progressions to the *cáscara* pattern. *However, this is only for practice and is not intended as a rhythmic pattern to be played consistently in a performance situation.*

Recommended Mode of Practice

1. Feeling the subdivision. **Play-Along Tracks 97-99**

It is extremely important for you to feel the subdivision in order to play with a consistent time feel. The very nature of playing and understanding syncopated rhythms depends on feeling the subdivisions.

In the following examples, I have written a steady single-note, eighth-note pattern with accents over the eighth notes that share the same beat or line up with the *cáscara*. By practicing these exercises from slow to fast, you will begin to feel the *cáscara* which will enable you to play with a consistent time feel.

2:3 SON CLAVE

3:2 SON CLAVE

CHAPTER 1 CLAVE, CÁSCARA, AND TUMBAO

2. *Cáscara* on for one bar and then off for the next bar. **Play-Along Tracks 101–107**

Once you have practiced the subdivision exercise, we can begin to practice by playing one bar of the *cáscara* and then playing the missing side of the *cáscara*. Remember to think about the subdivisions. Later on, you can think about the *tumbao* pattern.

CHAPTER 1   CLAVE, CÁSCARA, AND TUMBAO

3. Right Hand Independence. **Play-Along Tracks 109-111**

Put the *cáscara* (top line rhythm) in your fingers while you play the *clave* (bottom line rhythm) with your pick. If you are playing the example in fingerstyle: thumb for the *clave* and index, middle, and ring fingers for the *cáscara*. Then reverse the placement: *cáscara* in the thumb and *clave* in the index, middle, and ring fingers. Experiment with a muted sound in the fingers and a bass note in the thumb or vice versa.

CÁSCARA 2:3 SON PATTERN

CÁSCARA 3:2 SON PATTERN

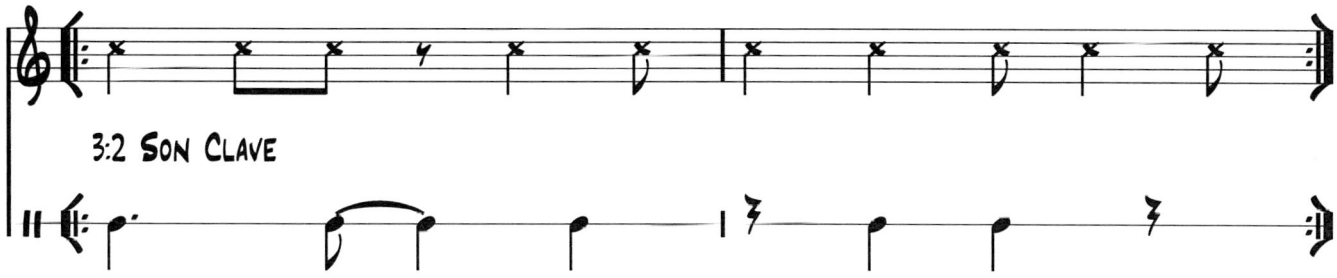

In order to get accustomed to playing the *cáscara*, we will now adapt various melodies with triadic/chordal qualities and well-known progressions to the pattern. This is the most fundamental rhythm for the execution of *guajeos* and *montunos*. Although the etudes begin

CHAPTER 1   CLAVE, CÁSCARA, AND TUMBAO

on the first beat, it is oftentimes varied and can be anticipated depending upon the harmonic, melodic and rhythmic content of the piece in question.

Each etude features a chord quality for two bars. One etude will be in 2:3 *clave* and the other in 3:2. Once you feel comfortable with the rhythmic pattern, try to substitute other notes and make your own *cáscara* lines.

These etudes are for practice and are not intended as a rhythmic pattern to be played over and over in a performance situation. But it will be valuable to practice either the pattern or variations of them for *guajeo*s, *montuno*s, comping and soloing. By practicing these etudes, it will help to plant the rhythm in your soul so that you can slowly understand how to vary it. In the next chapter, these same *cáscara* patterns will be converted to *guajeos/montunos*.

As you will see in the next chapter, the *cáscara* pattern is rhythmically varied to produce the basic rhythmic pattern of the *guajeo* and *montuno*. By utilizing the *cáscara* pattern in its original form, while holding the duration of the eighth-note over the rest, the etudes provide a simple variation of the *guajeo* and *montuno*. With that in mind, please don't be fooled into thinking that these exercises are the only variations of the *guajeo*s and *montuno*s. You can find more *guajeos* and *montunos* in Chapter 3.

In Chapters 6 and 7, the significance of the rhythmic use of the *cáscara* pattern in improvisation is explained, discussed, and is featured under each bar of the selected artist transcriptions.

CHAPTER 1　　　　　　　　　　　　　　　　　　　　　*CLAVE, CÁSCARA, AND TUMBAO*

Play-Along Tracks 113-119　　　　　　　　　　　*Suggested Position: V*

Single note Cáscara patterns starting from the root
Various chord qualities

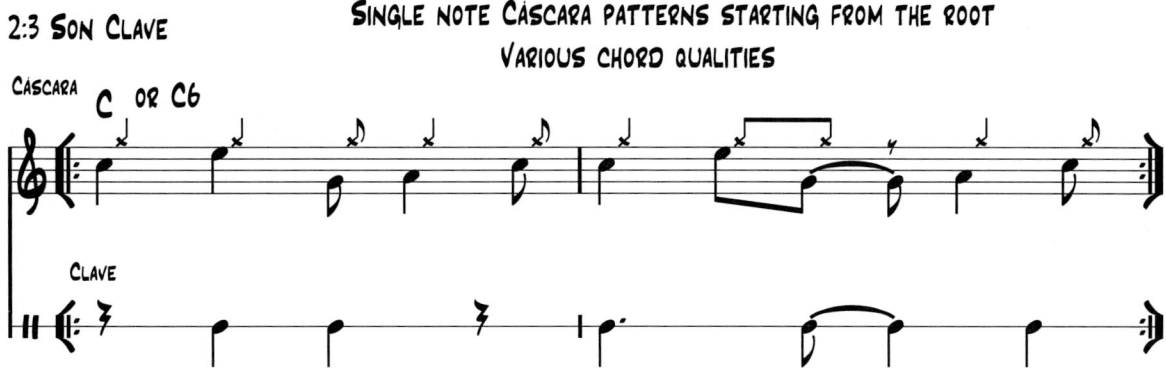

CONTEMPORARY LATIN JAZZ GUITAR, VOL. 1

CHAPTER 1

CLAVE, CÁSCARA, AND TUMBAO

Play-Along Tracks 121–127

Suggested Position: V

CHAPTER 1

CLAVE, CÁSCARA, AND TUMBAO

Play-Along Tracks 129-131

Suggested Position: V

CHAPTER 1

CLAVE, CÁSCARA, AND TUMBAO

Play-Along Tracks 133-139

Suggested Position: IV & V

CHAPTER 1

CLAVE, CÁSCARA, AND TUMBAO

Play-Along Tracks 141-145

Suggested Position: IV & V

CONTEMPORARY LATIN JAZZ GUITAR, VOL. 1

CHAPTER 1

CLAVE, CÁSCARA, AND TUMBAO

Play-Along Tracks 147-151

Suggested Position: IV & V

CHAPTER 1 — CLAVE, CÁSCARA, AND TUMBAO

Play-Along Tracks 153-159

Suggested Position: V

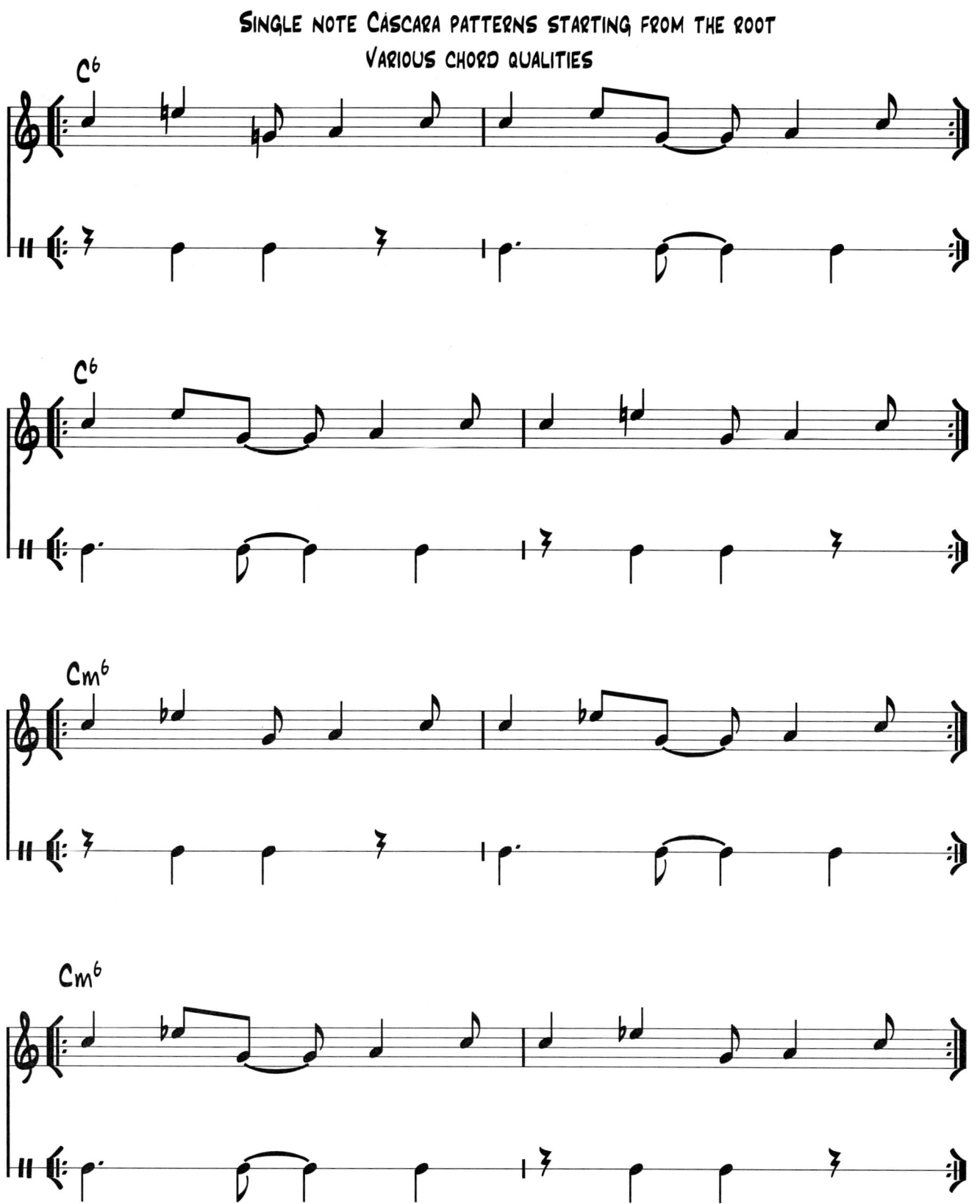

CONTEMPORARY LATIN JAZZ GUITAR, VOL. 1

CHAPTER 1

CLAVE, CÁSCARA, AND TUMBAO

Play-Along Tracks 161-167

Suggested Position: IV & V

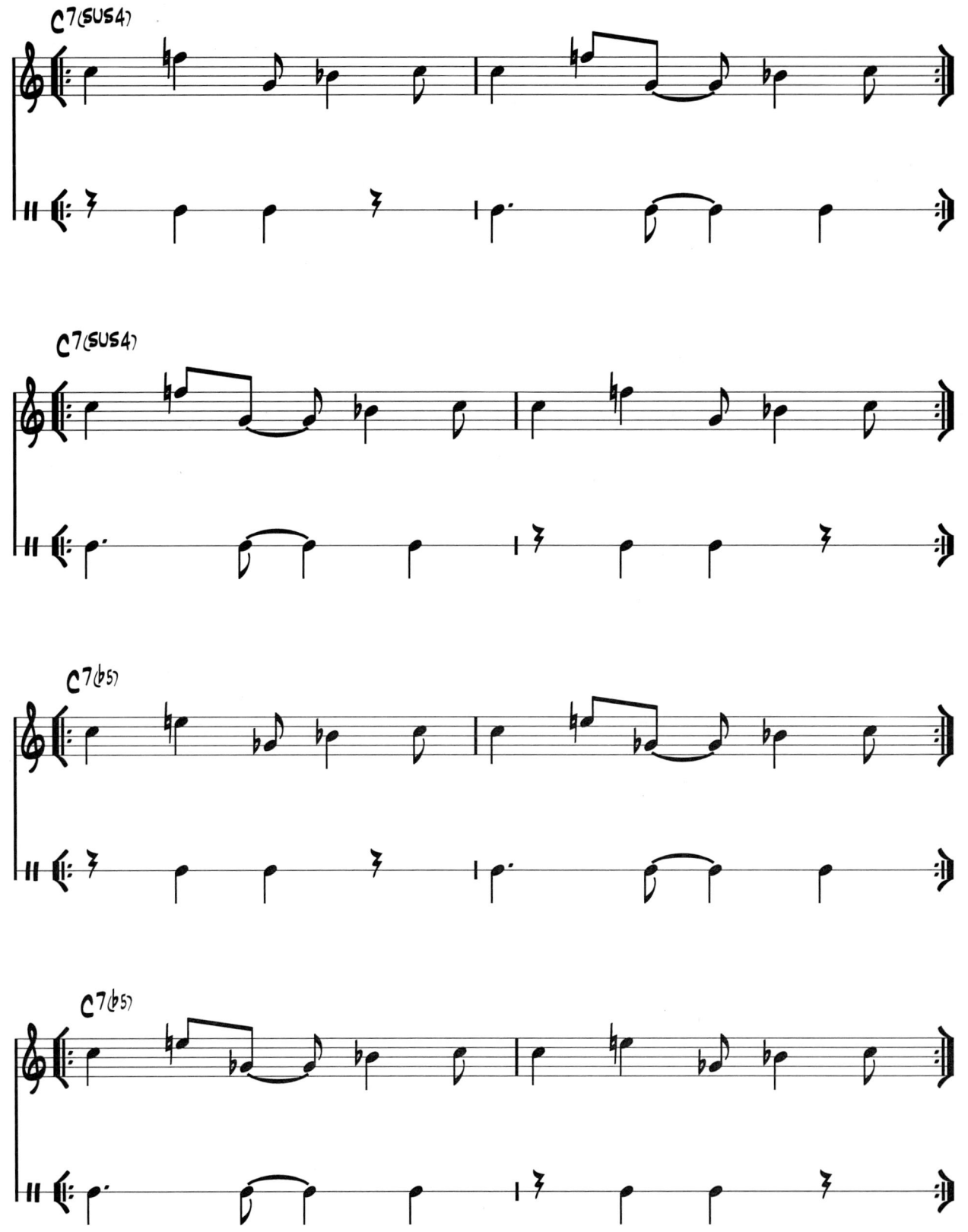

38   CONTEMPORARY LATIN JAZZ GUITAR, VOL. 1

CHAPTER 1

CLAVE, CÁSCARA, AND TUMBAO

Play-Along Tracks 169-175

Suggested Position: IV & V

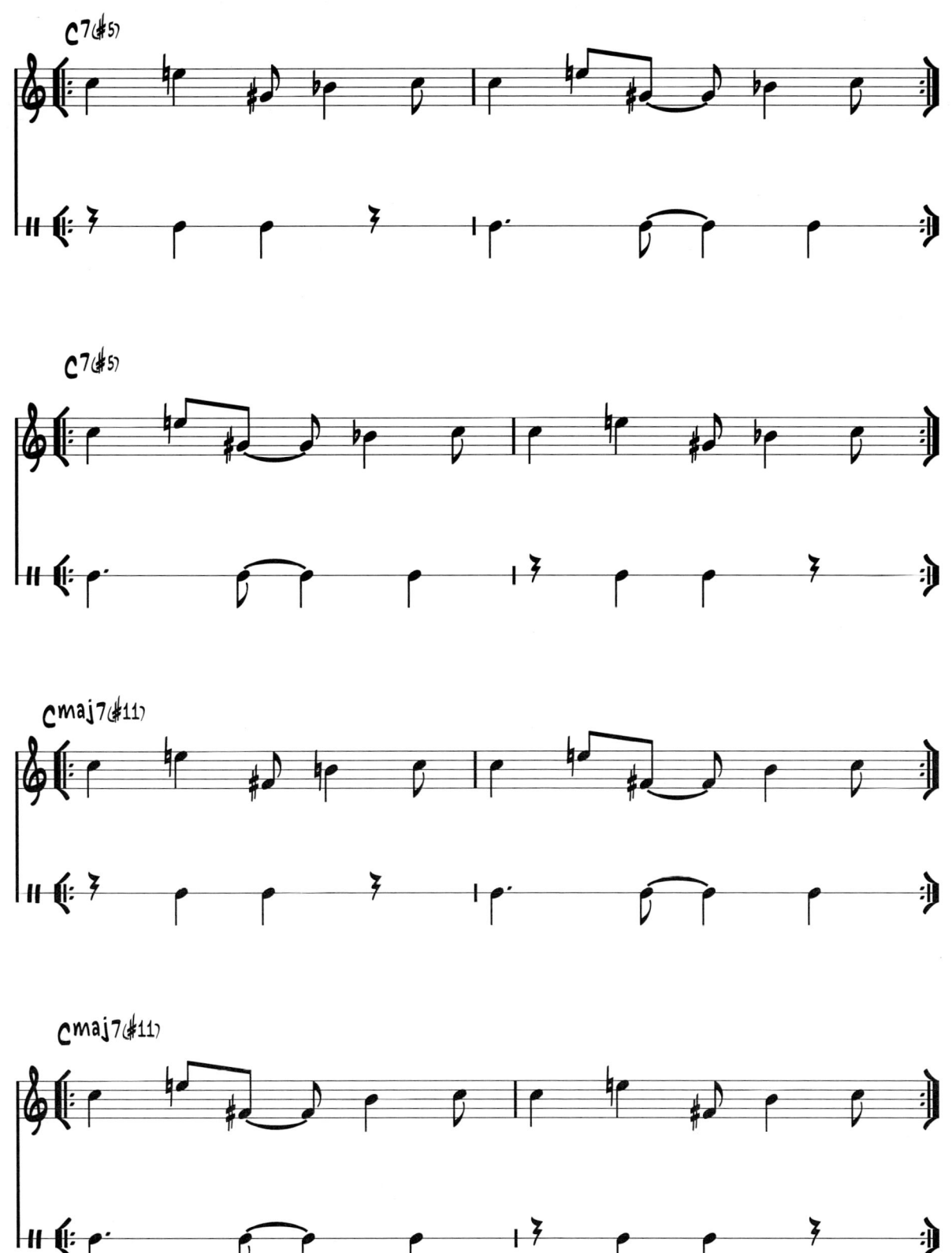

CONTEMPORARY LATIN JAZZ GUITAR, VOL. 1

CHAPTER 1   CLAVE, CÁSCARA, AND TUMBAO

Play-Along Tracks 177-183   *Suggested Position: IV & V*

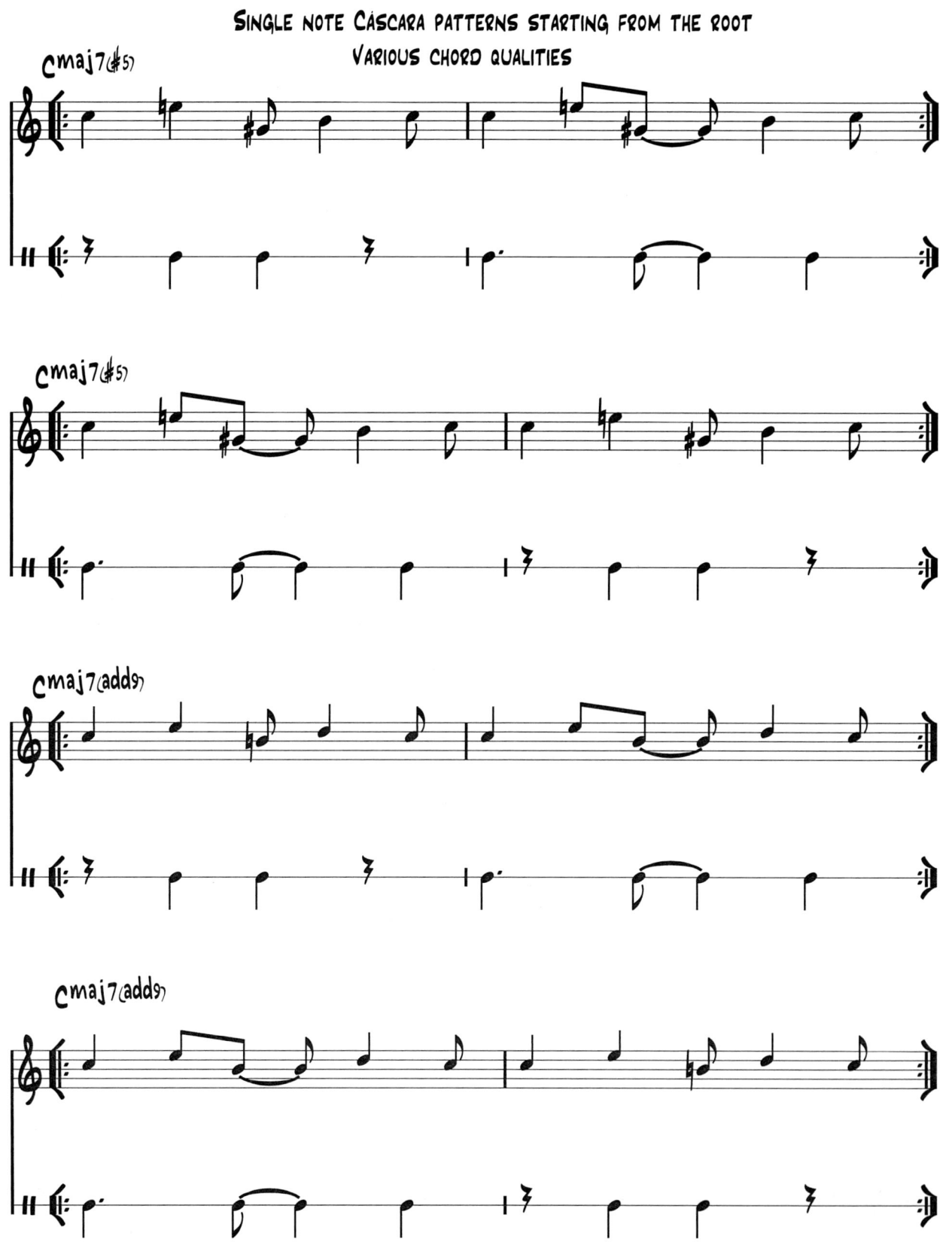

40   CONTEMPORARY LATIN JAZZ GUITAR, VOL. 1

CHAPTER 1 — CLAVE, CÁSCARA, AND TUMBAO

Play-Along Tracks 185-191 *Suggested Position: IV & V*

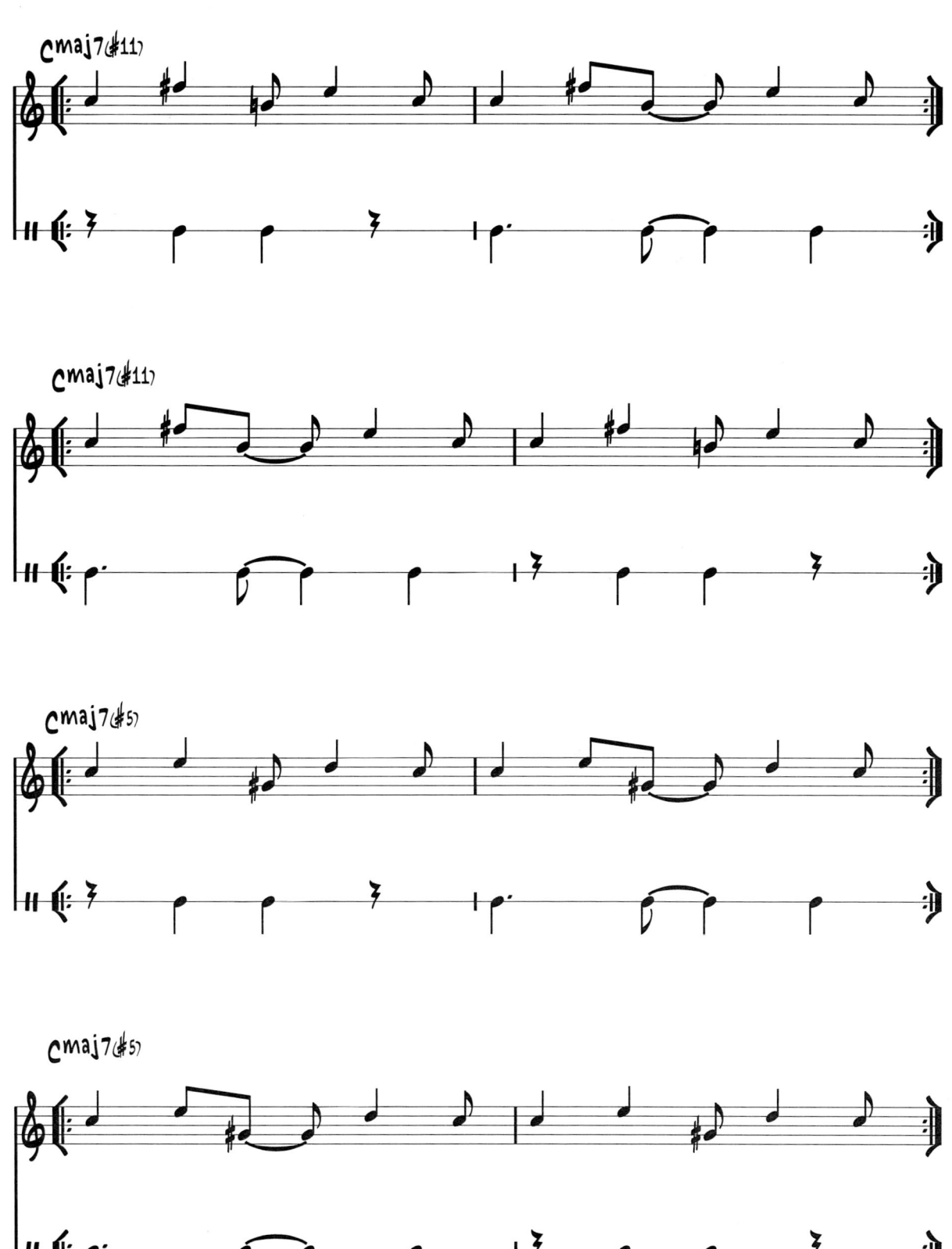

CONTEMPORARY LATIN JAZZ GUITAR, VOL. 1

CHAPTER 1
CLAVE, CÁSCARA, AND TUMBAO

Play-Along Tracks 193-199 *Suggested Position: IV*

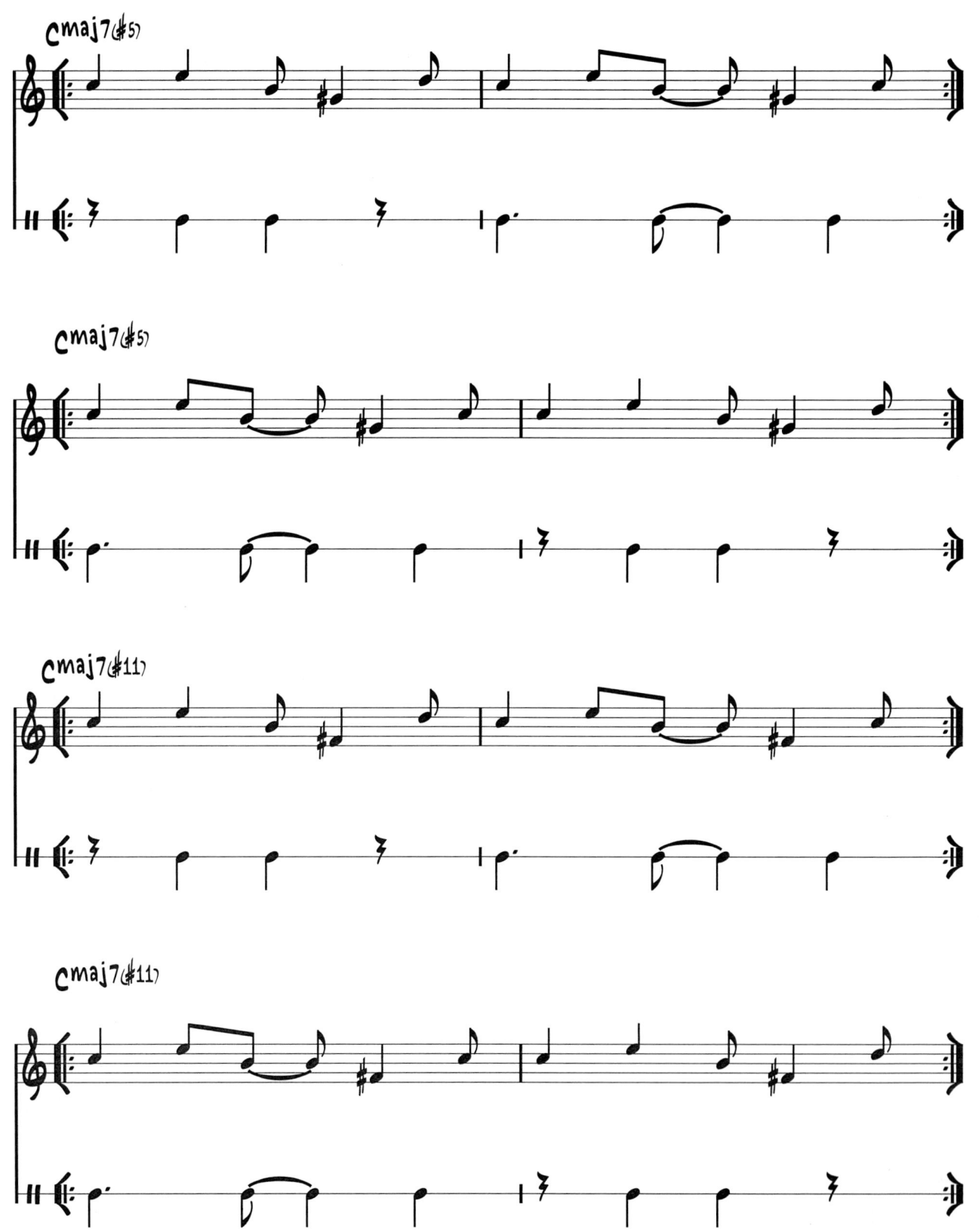

CONTEMPORARY LATIN JAZZ GUITAR, VOL. 1

Play-Along Tracks 201-207

Suggested Position: V

SINGLE NOTE CÁSCARA PATTERNS STARTING FROM THE ROOT
VARIOUS CHORD QUALITIES

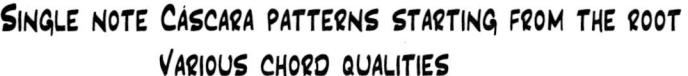

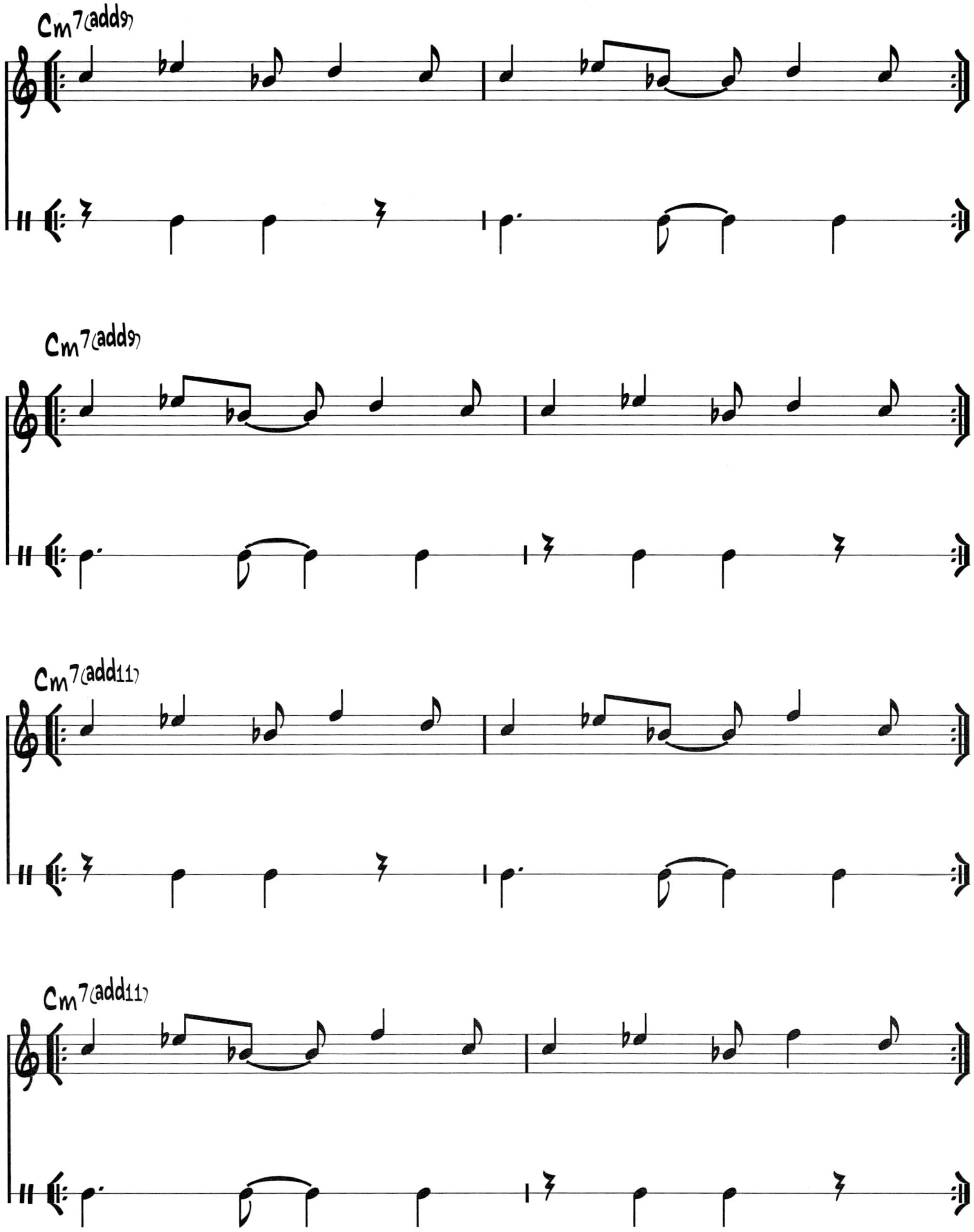

CHAPTER 1

CLAVE, CÁSCARA, AND TUMBAO

Play-Along Tracks 209-215

Suggested Position: V

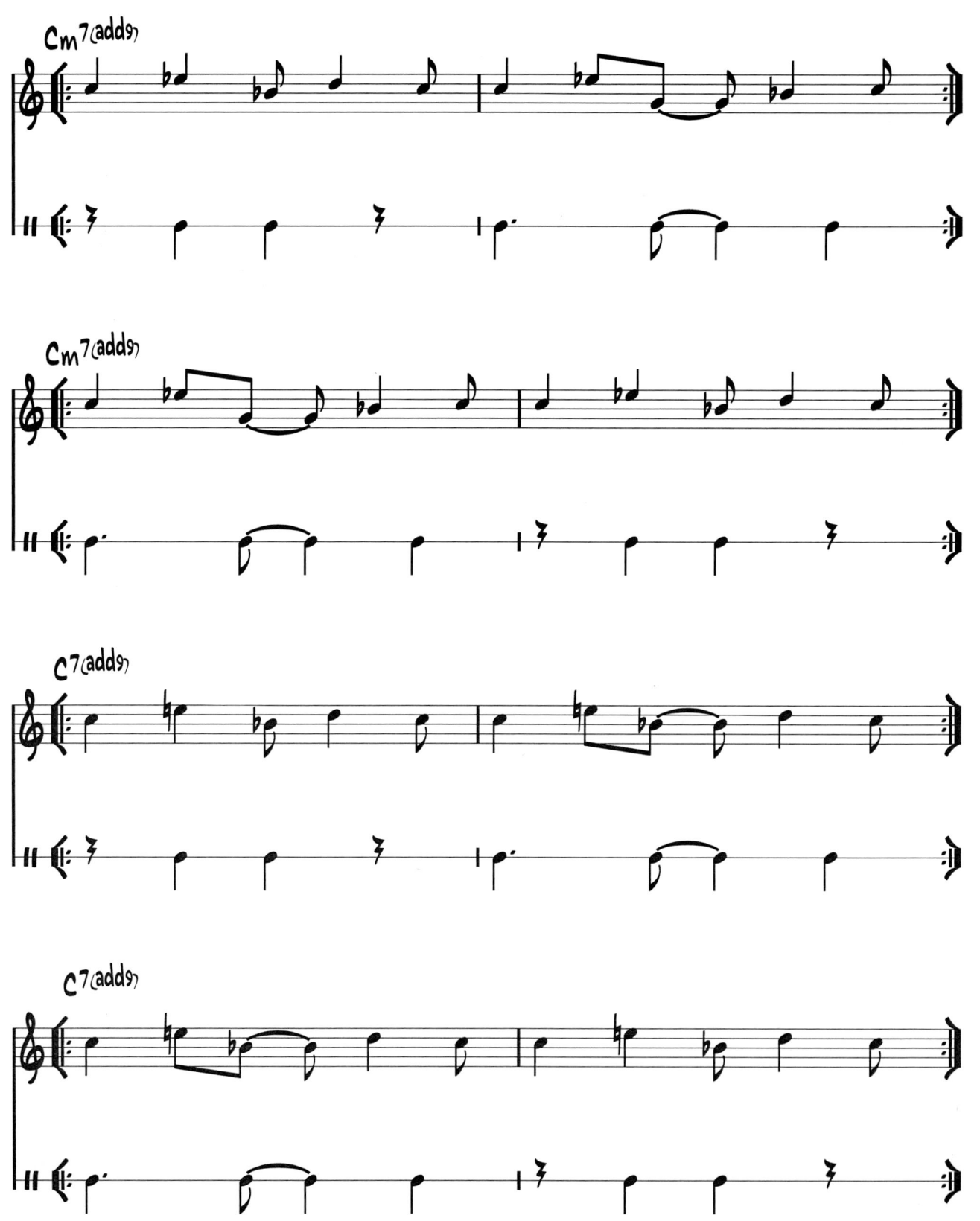

44

CONTEMPORARY LATIN JAZZ GUITAR, VOL. 1

CHAPTER 1 — CLAVE, CÁSCARA, AND TUMBAO

Play-Along Tracks 217-223 *Suggested Position: III*

CONTEMPORARY LATIN JAZZ GUITAR, VOL. 1

CHAPTER 1 — CLAVE, CÁSCARA, AND TUMBAO

Play-Along Tracks 225-231

Suggested Position: IV & V

SINGLE NOTE CÁSCARA PATTERNS STARTING FROM THE 5TH

CHAPTER 1 CLAVE, CÁSCARA, AND TUMBAO

Play-Along Tracks 233-239 *Suggested Position: III*

CHAPTER 1   CLAVE, CÁSCARA, AND TUMBAO

How did that feel? Did you try some of these patterns on one of your favorite songs? Did you try to improvise with the *cáscara* rhythm? Did you experiment with playing longer rhythmic durations that implied the *cáscara* rhythm? If not, these are all ideas worth spending some time on. Although the previous exercise resembles *guajeo*s and *montuno*s, they are only meant to outline the chord qualities using the *cáscara* rhythm. The ACTUAL *guajeo*s and *montuno*s are coming!

These etudes focused on single-note line interpretations of the *cáscara*. However, one can also apply this approach for comping, as exhibited in the next example by George Benson, as well as every other comping example in the book.

The broken vertical lines show how George Benson rhythmically articulates the *cáscara* pattern while executing the *clave* (solid vertical lines).

48   CONTEMPORARY LATIN JAZZ GUITAR, VOL. 1

CHAPTER 1   CLAVE, CÁSCARA, AND TUMBAO

Volume 2 of this series will show specific comping and soloing ideas that imply the *cáscara* pattern. However, please pay close attention to how each example contains the key rhythms, and how the melodic and harmonic aspects of each example align with *clave*, *cáscara*, and *tumbao*.

Tumbao

"The *tumbao* rhythm of the bass is a syncopated, repeating ostinato figure that is characterized by the 'and of beat 2' and 'beat 4.' Tumbaos tend to be constructed of one-bar cell patterns which do not conflict with the *clave*."[3]

A very important characteristic of the *tumbao* is that the roots of the chords are anticipated. This directly affects the harmony by anticipating chord changes either by an eighth note or a quarter note, as shown in the example above.

In solo, duo or trio settings without a bassist, the guitarist can play the *tumbao* pattern. If a bassist is present, the guitarist might sometimes anticipate the chords using the *tumbao* rhythm so that they do not conflict with it.

In order to get accustomed to playing *tumbao*, we will now practice the technique with *tumbao* and chords--and also anticipated chords. The following exercises are written to assist you in the assimilation of this technique. These *tumbao*s adapted for the guitar utilize different techniques such as:

- Arpeggiating the chord, which is also ergonomically easy to grab.
- Position-playing using large position jumps.
- A modern approach influenced by the piano.

---

[3] Rebeca Mauleón, *Salsa Guidebook for Piano and Ensemble* (Petaluma, CA: Sher Music, 1993).

CHAPTER 1 *CLAVE, CÁSCARA, AND TUMBAO*

Recommended Mode of Practice

1. Feeling the subdivisions. **Play-Along Track 241**

It is extremely important for you to feel the subdivision in order to play with a consistent time feel. The very nature of playing and understanding syncopated rhythms depends on feeling the subdivision.

In the following examples, I have written a steady eighth-note pattern with accents over the eighth notes that line up with the *tumbao*. By practicing these exercises from slow to fast, you will begin to feel the *tumbao* and enable yourself to play with rhythmic consistency.

2. *Tumbao* on for one bar and then off for the next bar. **Play-Along Tracks 243-245**

Once you have practiced the subdivision exercise, we can begin to practice by playing one bar of the *tumbao* and then playing the missing side of the *tumbao*. Remember to think about the subdivisions. Later on, you can think about all of the patterns and how they align rhythmically.

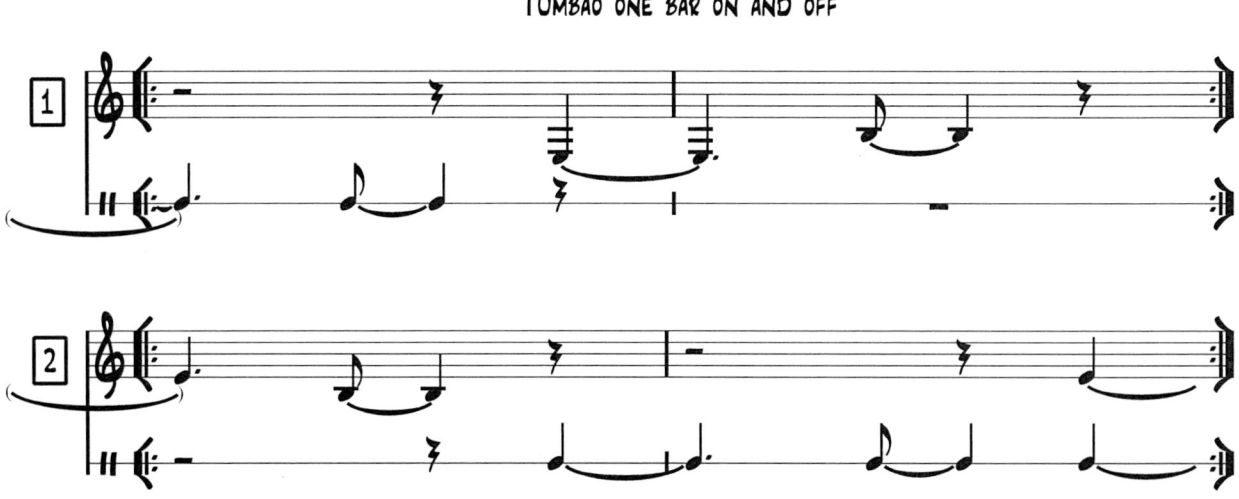

Have fun and adapt this technique to your favorite song.

CHAPTER 1   *CLAVE, CÁSCARA, AND TUMBAO*

Play-Along Tracks 247-251   *Suggested Position: I*

Chords and Tumbao with Variations

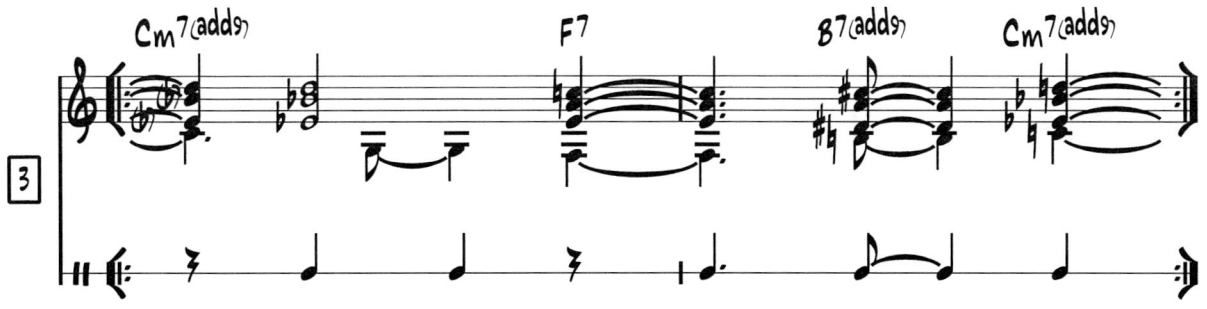

CONTEMPORARY LATIN JAZZ GUITAR, VOL. 1

CHAPTER 1

CLAVE, CÁSCARA, AND TUMBAO

Play-Along Tracks 253-261

Examples 4-7 Suggested Position: V Strings: 65432
Example 8 Suggested Position: V-III Strings: 5&2, 6&3

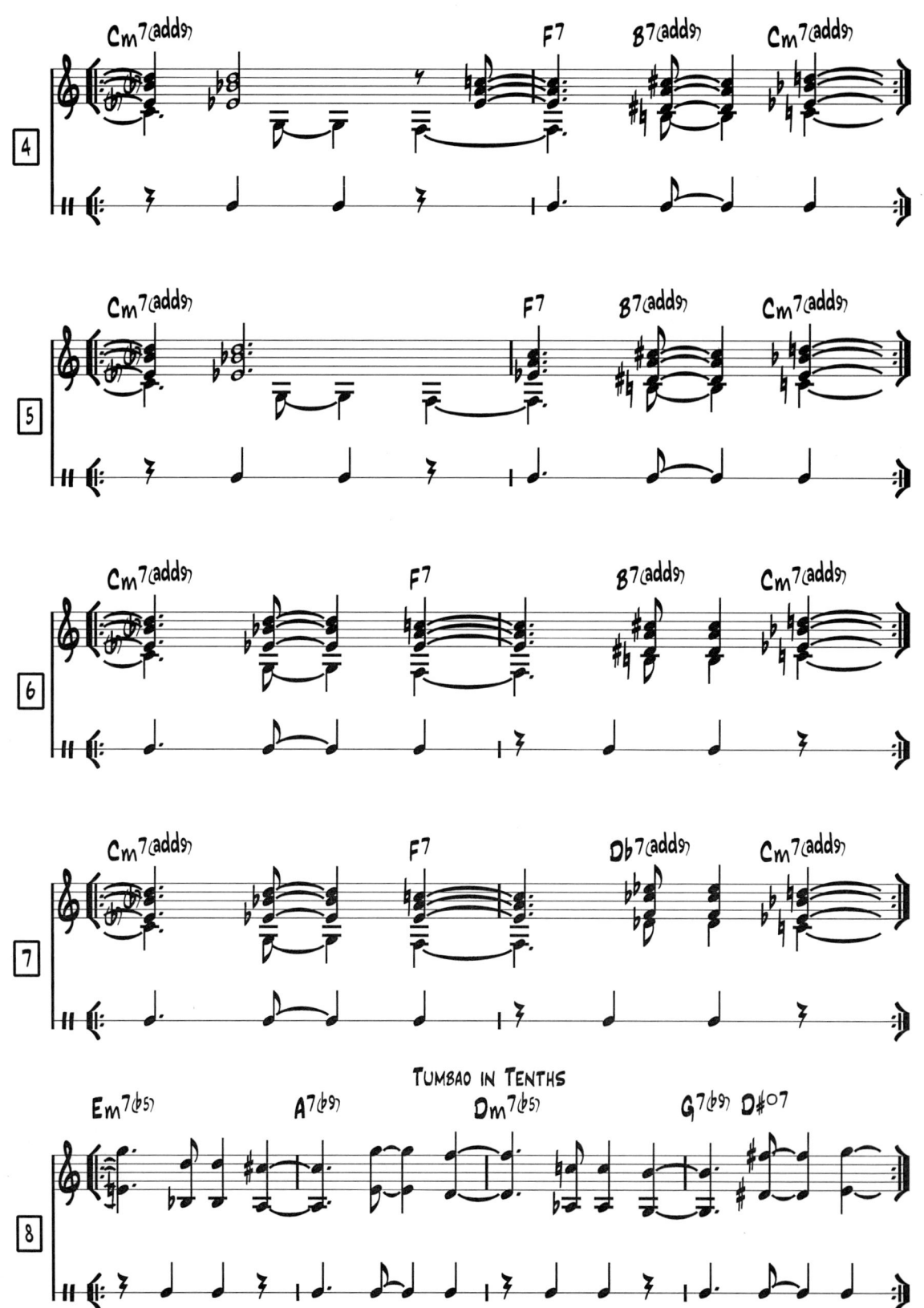

CHAPTER 1   *CLAVE, CÁSCARA, AND TUMBAO*

The next examples show some typical *tumbao* patterns by three guitarists, from traditional to contemporary formats.

CHAPTER 1 — CLAVE, CÁSCARA, AND TUMBAO

2:3 Son Clave

Richie Zellon "I Remember April" Guajeo 00:14–00:33

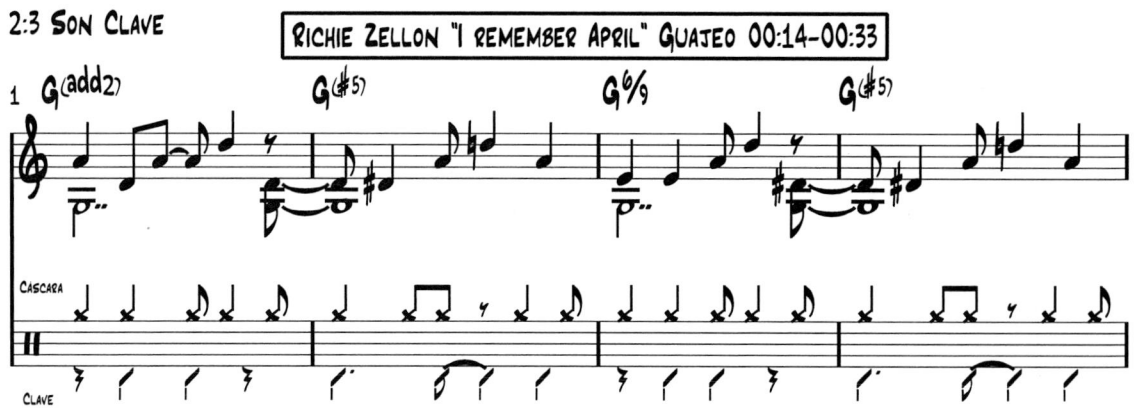

CHAPTER 1 — CLAVE, CÁSCARA, AND TUMBAO

Clave, *cáscara* and *tumbao* are the three rhythmic patterns (with many variations) that govern and determine how a player will phrase, interpret, and vary a rhythm within Latin music. In the following chapters, each musical example will make reference to the *clave*, *cáscara* and *tumbao* by including the rhythm above or below the staff. The reference to these rhythms in turn, and their connection to the example, help to fortify your knowledge and comprehension by explaining the correlations between them.

Here's one last example to wrap up the section.

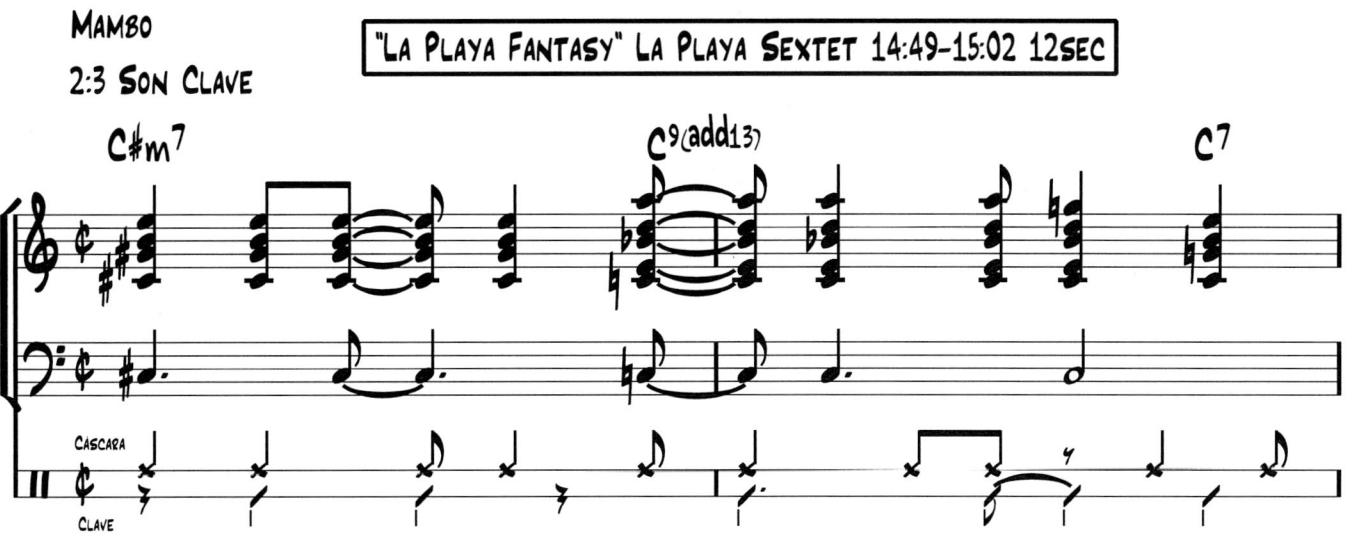

CONTEMPORARY LATIN JAZZ GUITAR, VOL. 1

CHAPTER 1 CLAVE, CÁSCARA, AND TUMBAO

In "La Playa Fantasy" by La Playa Sextet, Paul Alicea plays the melody of the song in a standard chord melody fashion consistent with the techniques used by Jazz guitarists of the period. Notice the variation of drop two, drop three and quartal voicings throughout. The melody demonstrates how the melodic and harmonic rhythm played by Paul Alicea and the horns line up and vary with both the *clave*, *cáscara*, and *tumbao* rhythms too.

Bars 1 and 3 clearly outline the cascara pattern while bars 2 and 4 show alignment with the *clave* and a brief alignment with the *cáscara*. On the two side of the *clave*, Alicea's melodic rhythm figure only lines up with the first quarter note of the *clave* pattern. However, the melodic rhythm does adhere to the *cáscara* rhythm almost exactly with exception to the first eighth note on beat two of the two side of the *clave*. Bars 5, 7, 9, 11-12 are interesting because the melodic rhythm lines up with the downbeat and anticipation of the *tumbao* rhythm consistent with the style of mambo. Bars 6, 8, and 10 offer alignment with the last

CHAPTER 1   CLAVE, CÁSCARA, AND TUMBAO

quarter note on the three side of the *clave*. Bars 11 is interesting because it shows how the rhythmic figure lines up with the anticipation of the eighth note figure of the *tumbao* in the first half of the bar while aligning with the *cáscara* on the quarter and eighth note.

CHAPTER 2
Guajeos and *Montunos*

As we saw in the previous Chapter, *clave, cáscara,* and bass *tumbao* are the fundamental rhythmic elements that shape our role as a Latin jazz guitarist. These elements rhythmically support how a *guajeo, montuno,* or *tumbao* functions in Afro-Cuban music and Latin jazz. Chapter 2 is dedicated to showing the relationship between these elements and the *guajeo/montuno*.

In order to understand this rhythmic relationship, each musical example will include the *clave, cáscara,* and *tumbao*. The proper execution of a *guajeo* and *montuno* lies solely on the realization of the rhythmic similarities with the *clave, cáscara* and *tumbao*. Therefore, while still accomplishing an independent harmonic and rhythmic layer, it is stylistically consistent with the definition of a *guajeo* and *montuno*. Through note choice and rhythmic variation, these two layers create two unique characteristics that are essential.

The *guajeo* is the repeated figure that is played by the string instruments in a particular ensemble such as the *tres* vamp in a *conjunto* instrumentation.[1] The *guajeo* pattern is a single or harmonized note sequence that can accentuate and vary the *clave, cáscara* and *tumbao* pattern in a one to two-bar phrase. This harmonized note sequence utilizes the chord tones (root, 3rd, 5th or 7th) in an arpeggiated or varied pattern while accentuating the *clave* to establish a harmonic foundation. Below are some classic examples of two-bar *guajeo* patterns that utilize the triads to produce harmonic stability.

---

1   Mauleón, Rebeca. *Salsa Guidebook for Piano and Ensemble, Sher Music co,* (Petaluma, CA: Sher Music, 1999). The *guajeo* is also played by saxophones and other instruments in a big band context. Listen to Tito Puente or Machito.

CHAPTER 2

GUAJEOS AND MONTUNOS

The *clave* affects the *guajeo* and *montuno* in the following ways:

- All two-bar *guajeos* or *montunos* must reflect the downbeat and syncopation of the *clave* by accentuating the downbeat or quarter note on the 2 side of the *clave* (marked in solid vertical lines), and the syncopation or eighth note tied to quarter note on the 3 side (marked in solid vertical lines).

- A one-bar phrase doesn't adhere to this rule as seen in the top line of the example.

- It is also important to note how the *tumbao* of the bass and the *cáscara* support the *clave*, *guajeo* and *montuno* (marked in broken vertical lines).

Track 263   2:3 Son Clave #1

CONTEMPORARY LATIN JAZZ GUITAR, VOL. 1

CHAPTER 2 GUAJEOS AND MONTUNOS

Track 265 3:2 Son Clave #2

The examples above show two of the many *guajeo* and *montuno* rhythmic variations possible. However, please pay attention to how each player uses articulation and dynamics to create their own unique melodic and rhythmic variations of the *guajeo* and *montuno*.

CHAPTER 2 — GUAJEOS AND MONTUNOS

Arsenio Rodríguez displays a *guajeo* constructed upon the chord tones of B♭min in bars 1 and 3 and F7 in bars 2 and 4. Notice how he begins his note choice for the B♭min *guajeo* with Rt ♭3 5 and, because of voice leading, his note choice for the F7 is logically the nearest note as in bars 2 to 3. However, bar 4 is a direct sequence of the original motif that starts in bar 2 as shown in brackets.

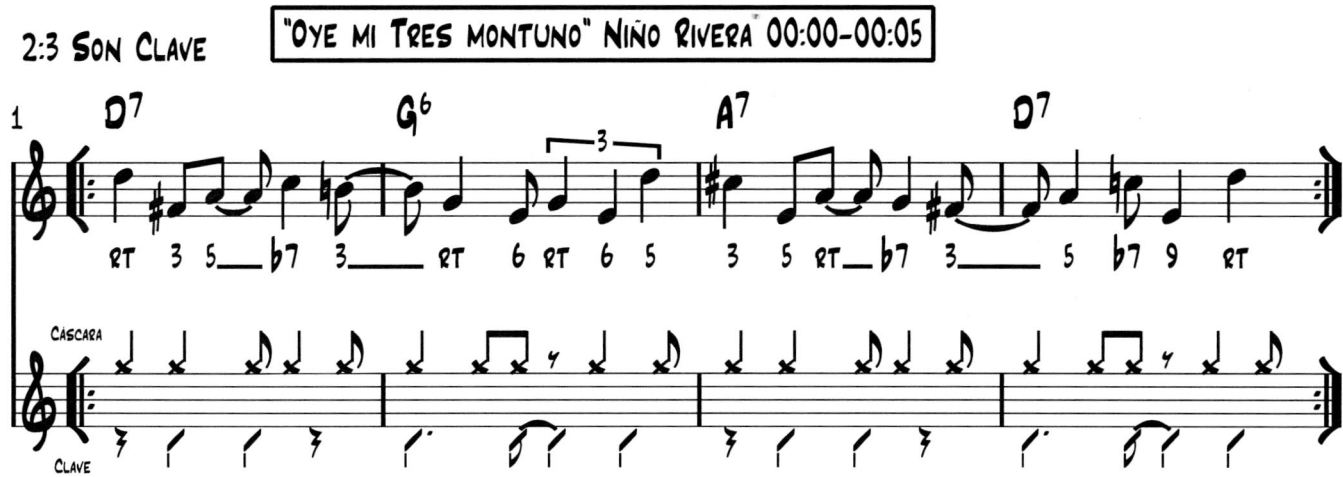

El Niño Rivera outlines a D7 chord in bar 1 while voice-leading the 7th (C) (as an anticipation and therefore agreeing with the *clave*) to the 3rd of G6. Bar 3 outlines A7 and begins with a C♯, the 3rd, to outline the A7 chord (A C♯ E G) and anticipates the 3rd of the D7 chord (F♯) to end the phrase.

In the next example, we have Nelson González playing a *montuno* in 2:3 *rumba clave* on "Trompeta en Cuero" with Grupo Folklorico y Experimental Nuevayorquino on the album *Lo Dice Todo* (1976).

CHAPTER 2 — GUAJEOS AND MONTUNOS

Notice how Nelson outlines the basic triads of the chords while conforming to the *cáscara* in bars 1 & 3. It is interesting to note that in bars 1 and 3, the G and F# rhythmically line up with the first beat of the two side of the *clave*.

Montuno is the repeated syncopated pattern played by the piano in an ensemble.[2] The term *"montuno"* is also used for a piano *guajeo*, the ostinato figure accompanying the *montuno* section. Piano adaptations of the *tres guajeo* can be extraordinarily intricate and syncopated. Because the piano player makes use of two hands, the pianist has more freedom to interpret the *guajeos* with more harmony and can even play the bass *tumbaos* as well.

Piano *Montuno*

Source: Mauleón-Santana, Rebeca. "The Heart of Salsa." Keyboard, January 1996.

Guajeos and *montunos* can also be one-bar phrases. These repetitive one-bar figures are *clave* neutral, meaning that they do not support or reinforce any particular *clave*. Here are some basic one-bar *guajeo/montuno* examples:

---

2 Source: Mauleón-Santana, Rebeca. "The Heart of Salsa." Keyboard, January 1996.

CHAPTER 2   GUAJEOS AND MONTUNOS

Tracks 267-269 *Guajeos/Montunos*, One Bar Phrase #1

2:3 Son Clave

3:2 Son Clave

Tracks 271-273 *Guajeos/Montunos*, One Bar Phrase #2

2:3 Son Clave

3:2 Son Clave

CHAPTER 2   GUAJEOS AND MONTUNOS

The next examples are some basic two-bar *montuno* patterns derived from the earlier exercises written in the *cáscara* section. The differences happen in bar 1, with the downbeat on beat 2 and with the anticipation of beat 3 by an eighth-note. Bar two is then anticipated by an eighth-note as well.

Track 275 *Cáscara* Rhythmic Exercise #1

Track 277 *Guajeo* Conversion #1

Track 279 *Cáscara* Rhythmic Exercise #2

64   CONTEMPORARY LATIN JAZZ GUITAR, VOL. 1

CHAPTER 2　　　　　　　　　　　　　　　　　　　　　GUAJEOS AND MONTUNOS

Tracks 281 & 283　*Guajeo* Conversion (#1 & #2)

Once you have analyzed and identified the differences between the examples, then you can change the earlier exercises into *guajeos* and *montunos*.

Guajeo, *montuno*, or *tumbao* are the names for the ostinato patterns that are played by the *tres*, *cuatro*, *requinto*, and piano. The adaptation of *tres*, *cuatro* and piano *guajeos* and *montunos* to the guitar are executed by using single-note, intervallic and chordal techniques. The success of these techniques is based upon harmonic transparency, amplification and sometimes effects like overdrive or chorus.

The single-note technique is the simplest and most commonly used method because it doesn't employ intervals or intervallic structures such as triads or clusters. As the name states, the guitarist only plays single-note patterns on the *guajeo/montuno* rhythm, as demonstrated by Paul Alicea and La Playa Sextet in the following examples.

CHAPTER 2 — GUAJEOS AND MONTUNOS

2:3 Son Clave — "Mambo Batiri" La Playa Sextet 0:55–0:59

2:3 Son Clave — "Running-runnin" La Playa Sextet 0:03–0:11

CHAPTER 2

GUAJEOS AND MONTUNOS

2:3 Son Clave — "Coco Seco" La Playa Sextet 0:09–0:56

CHAPTER 2   *GUAJEOS* AND *MONTUNOS*

Although the single-note technique resembles what a *tres or cuatro* would play, it doesn't have the same sound because of one crucially important detail: both instruments have doubled strings that are tuned to octaves or in unison and are higher pitched. However, if a guitarist manages to have a big enough sound (stereo, effects, EQ, overdrive, etc.) then the single-note technique can be very effective in providing contrast to the various sections.

The intervallic technique is a combination of intervals that favors the guitar's tuning. This technique can be used either with one guitarist or two guitarists. It is also a series or combination of any interval that is technically executable at a given tempo and key. Usually, octaves, thirds, sixths and minor tenths are most commonly used. However, in Latin jazz any series or combination of intervals can be used. In most cases, arrangers and composers used two guitarists to achieve the same sound of *tres* and *cuatro*. Let's take a look at that.

CHAPTER 2 GUAJEOS AND MONTUNOS

La Playa Sextet and the rival band La Plata Sextette, featuring Paul Alicea and Frankie Sánchez, used two guitarists to achieve this technique. The next example shows how Paul Alicea and Frankie Sánchez (of La Playa Sextet) employ an innovative approach of using two guitars, harmonizing the *guajeo* in fifths, sixths and octaves.

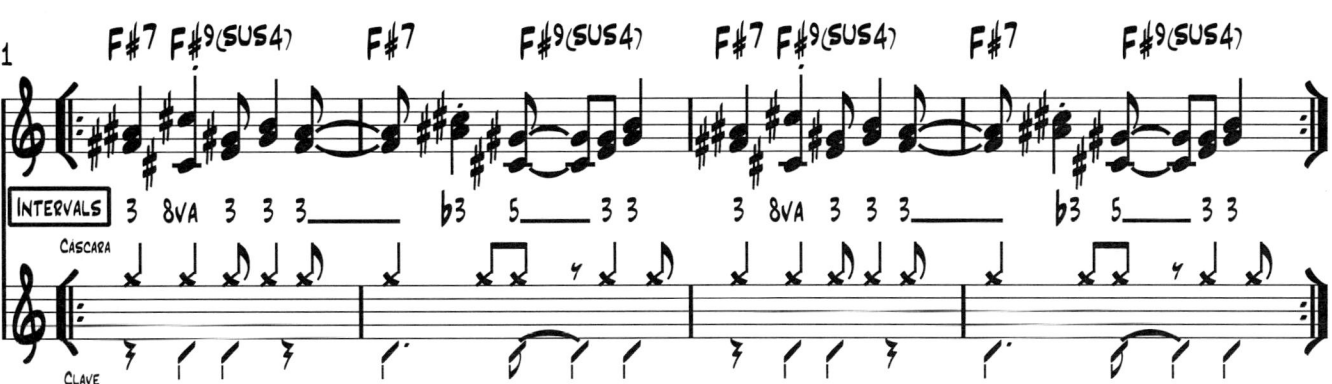

CONTEMPORARY LATIN JAZZ GUITAR, VOL. 1

CHAPTER 2 — GUAJEOS AND MONTUNOS

Stan Appelbaum and Chico O'Farrill arranged two guitars in the following ways:

This previous example shows how arranger Stan Appelbaum arranged and orchestrated "Leyte" for Cal Tjader's record *Breeze From the East*. Applebaum creates a *guajeo*-like figure for the two guitars that is harmonized in a way that is reminiscent of Clare Fischer's composing style[3]. This technique of harmonizing using non-traditional intervals gives a modern sound more inclined to the jazz side of Latin jazz. It's also important to point out that this recording featured vibraphone, guitars, strings, bass and percussion without piano (!).

---

3 Please visit www.clarefischer.com for more information.

CHAPTER 2

GUAJEOS AND MONTUNOS

In the previous example, O'Farrill writes a *guajeo* in 2:3 *son clave*. The *guajeo* is then harmonized for two guitarists (Barry Galbraith and Everett Barksdale) in bar 5, creating contrary motion counterpoint that starts from unison, 2nds and 3rds to the tritone of the F#7 on beat 3 in bar 6. O'Farrill repeats the same figure while changing the ending of the two-bar phrase in bar 8.

In the next example, Clare Fischer featured the guitar of Danny Embrey as an ensemble instrument blending with the piano *montuno* in the following manner, on the cha-cha-chá in 2:3 *son clave* entitled "Pavillón," from 2:49-3:05 on the album *Crazy Bird*.

CHAPTER 2 GUAJEOS AND MONTUNOS

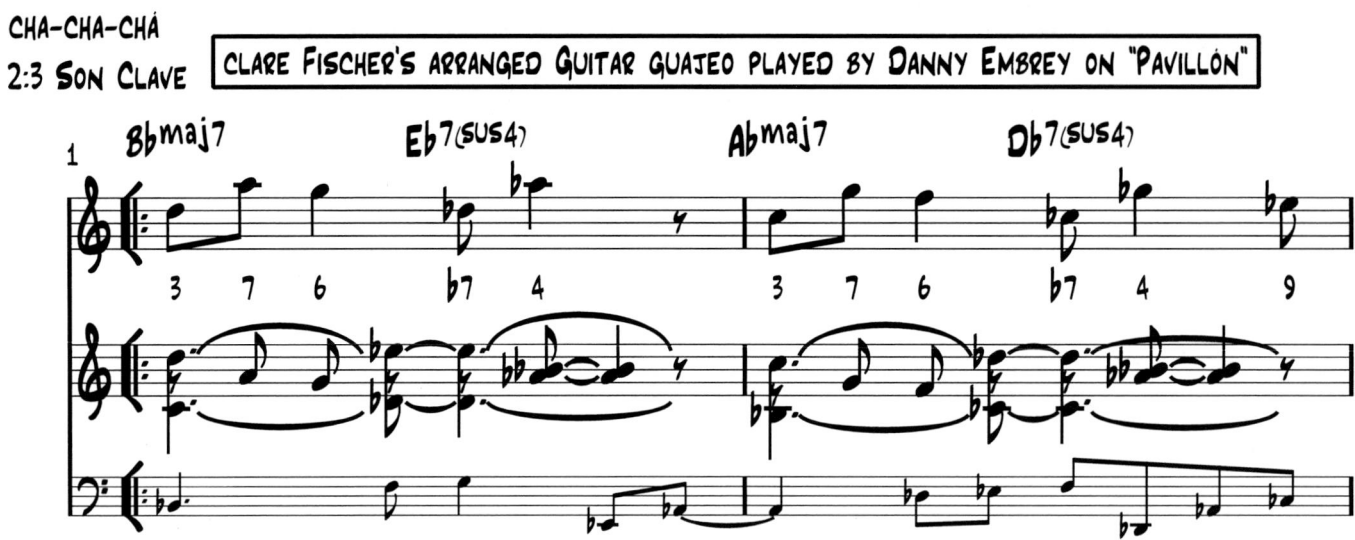

Notice how Clare arranged Danny's guitar with emphasis on the 3rd, 7ths and tensions of 6 and sus 4. This is a modern departure from the triadic concept emphasized in the traditional *guajeos* and *montunos* in the previous chapters.

On the next example from Cal Tjader's *Breeze From the East* recording of "Leyte," we see Jimmy Raney playing an arranged comping part on a cha-cha-chá. This example demonstrates the alternation between single-note guide tones and a chordal structure. In essence, Appelbaum creates yet another unique version of the common comping rhythm for the style, which is similar to the piano intro on "Morning" by Clare Fischer.

CHAPTER 2

GUAJEOS AND MONTUNOS

However, Paul Alicea, Sonny Henry, Edgardo Miranda, Steve Khan and other modern guitarists achieved this with one guitar. The following examples show how the guitarists used a combination of single lines, intervals, triads, clusters and chords. Please feel free to play along with the examples.

CONTEMPORARY LATIN JAZZ GUITAR, VOL. 1

CHAPTER 2 GUAJEOS AND MONTUNOS

Sonny Henry doubled the piano part in "Adobo Criollo" because of the necessity to blend the instruments together. However, in Willie Bobo's group, Sonny Henry's guitar is the principal harmonic and accompaniment instrument. His part on "Sham Time" features chords and the doubling of the bass line on beats 3 and 4 of the B♭7. This part gives way to the *guajeo* pattern, outlining the anticipated guide-tones and chordal structures that are conveniently available (on strings 432) to the guitarist in bars 1 and 2.

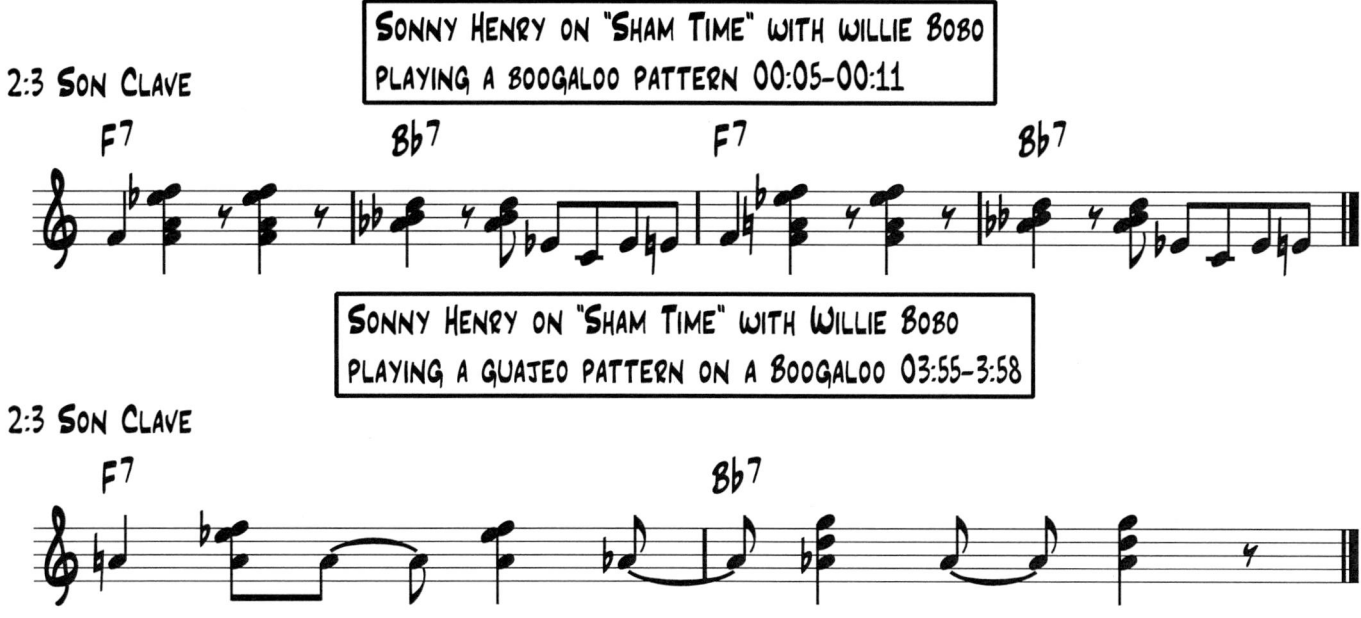

In the next example, we see how Steve Khan arranges a *montuno* for guitar on McCoy Tyner's "Hymn Song."

CHAPTER 2 — GUAJEOS AND MONTUNOS

Notice how Steve alternates between triads and quartal voicings (bar 4 brackets) for a more sophisticated sounding *montuno*. Steve's comping and improvisational style is highlighted later with his fantastic solo on "Gracinha."

The next example features Richie Zellon executing a traditional *montuno* in bars 1-2 on the jazz standard "I'll Remember April." The second example offers a *montuno* using characteristics similar to what Sonny Henry employed.

CHAPTER 2 GUAJEOS AND MONTUNOS

2:3 SON CLAVE

2:3 SON CLAVE

In the next example a modern application of intervals and harmony is applied to a traditional *guajeo* pattern over a *bomba*. Notice the alternations between 7ths and 2nds, and 7ths and 6ths throughout the example.

Track 285 "Adelante" by Neff Irizarry *Suggested Position: VI-IX*

76 CONTEMPORARY LATIN JAZZ GUITAR, VOL. 1

CHAPTER 2

GUAJEOS AND MONTUNOS

Track 287 "Dulcito de Coco" Guajeo Adaptation *Suggested Position: V & VI*

The *guajeo* adaptation for the song "Dulcito de Coco" by Vicente García displays my own use of more sophisticated techniques that highlight parallel intervals, chord voicings and single lines. Bar 1 highlights 6th intervals on the Amin7 chord that voice-lead to the F/C chord.

Bar 2 continues with chord voicings that contrapuntally open up to a single-note pickup (E) to the interval of the min 6th, which are pickups to the repetition of the figure. The A section, at bar 5, displays cluster intervals mixed with single-notes that are similar to the style of Steve Khan.

"Chucho" displays yet another re-adaptation of the standard *guajeo*, using a combination of octaves and single-note lines that outline the given harmony. This *guajeo* adaptation also highlights the anticipation of the harmony following the *tumbao* pattern by one beat, as seen in bar 4 with the anticipation of the minor 3rd of the Gmin7 chord on beat 4. Bar

CHAPTER 2 — GUAJEOS AND MONTUNOS

4 also shows a reharmonization of the *guajeo* using the upper structure (C b3rd, Eb b5th, G b7) instead of the root triad of Amin7b5 (A Rt, C b3rd Eb b5th).

Track 289 "Chucho" *Guajeo* Adaptation *Suggested Positions: V-XI, Strings:321*

CHAPTER 2 — GUAJEOS AND MONTUNOS

This example shows a *montuno* pattern over Paquito D'Rivera's composition "Chucho." This piece is a Latin jazz standard and always a challenge to play over.

Here's an etude that displays how the *guajeo*, *clave* and *tumbao* patterns can be played on the guitar on a B♭ blues entitled "Virginiarican Blues." In this example, I make use of a combination of upper-structure voicings, standard drop-two voicings, and *guajeo* patterns in the first line guitar part. The second guitar part plays drop-three style voicings using the *tumbao* pattern that establishes the harmonic foundation for the first guitar part to function. Notice the drop-two voicings played in *clave* that give way to a *guajeo* pattern; this section features compound intervals including minor 10ths and 2nds over the E♭9 chord in measure 5, while voice-leading the same pattern on the and of beat 2 with a minor 10th moving to a minor 3rd over the Edim7 chord.

CHAPTER 2 GUAJEOS AND MONTUNOS

Track 291

Suggested Position indicated with Roman numerals

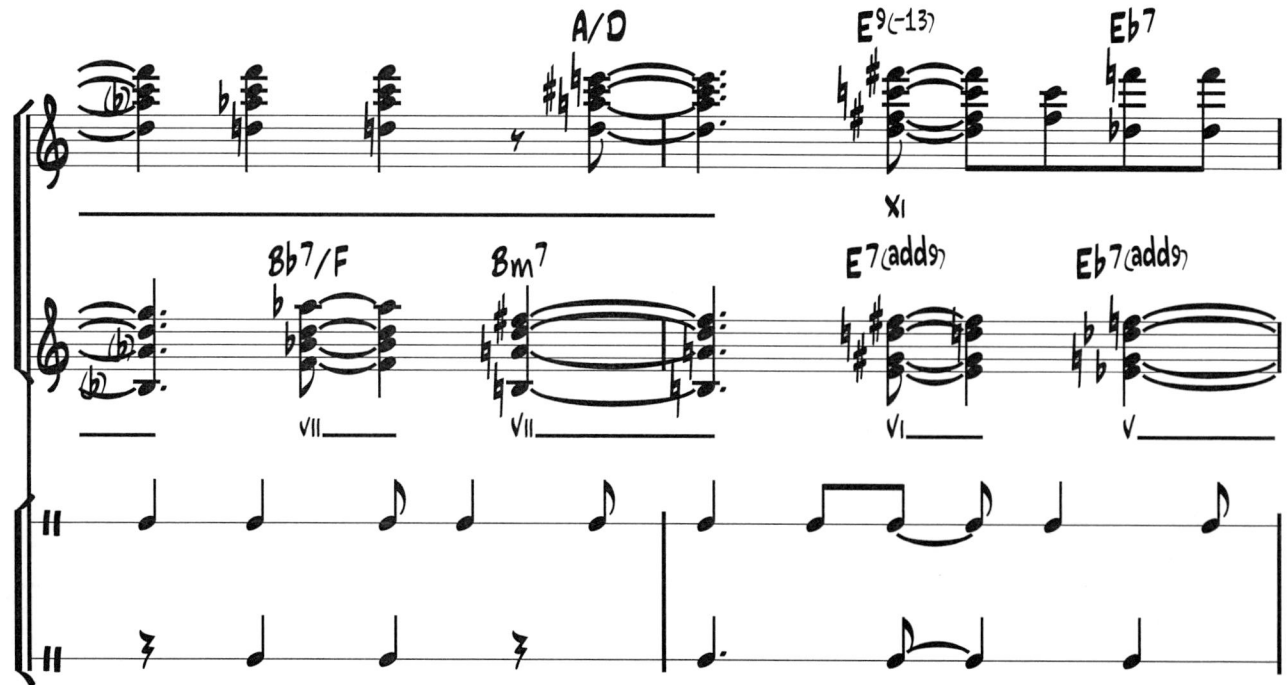

80 CONTEMPORARY LATIN JAZZ GUITAR, VOL. 1

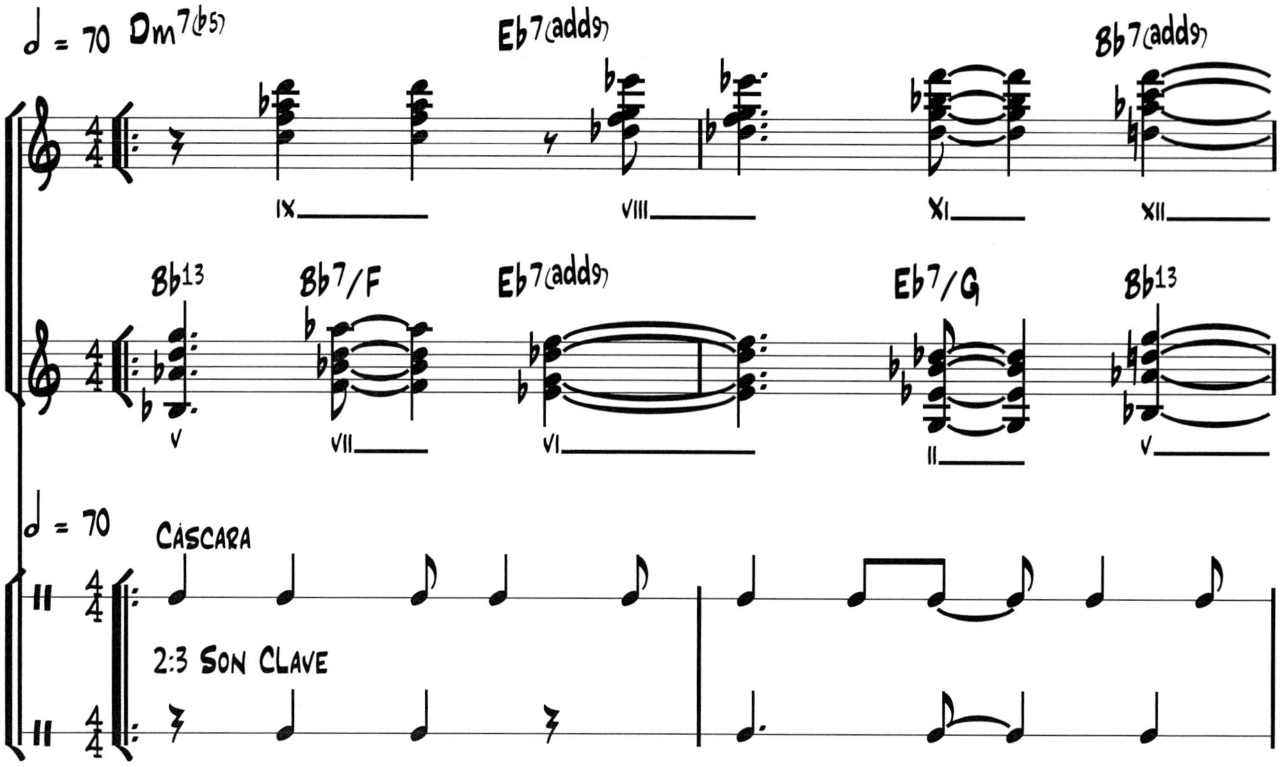

CHAPTER 2 GUAJEOS AND MONTUNOS

CONTEMPORARY LATIN JAZZ GUITAR, VOL. 1

CHAPTER 2 *GUAJEOS* AND *MONTUNOS*

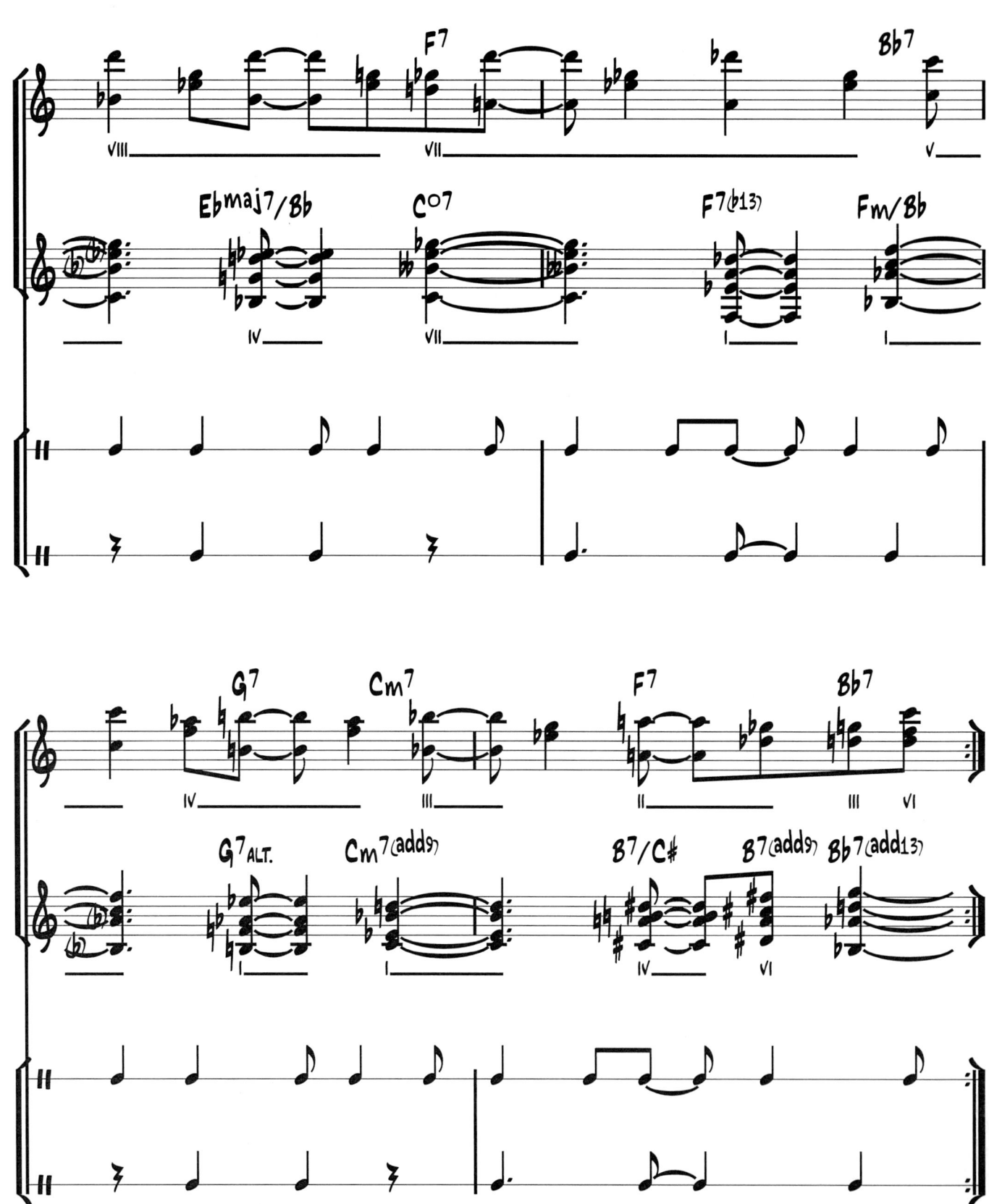

CHAPTER 2   GUAJEOS AND MONTUNOS

I have included "Virginiarican Blues" again in Chapter 8 so that you can play through it from a different perspective.

The previous re-adaptions represent my unique creative interpretation of the traditional instruments as well as the piano, and most importantly, the pioneering contributions of the legendary Latin jazz guitarists in the field, to provide you with some solutions on how to play guitar in Latin jazz. However, I have included on the last two pages of this Chapter a reference sheet and one more artist example. Finally, once you have read through the next chapters in the book, I suggest that you revisit this section again.

The last example, "La Cáscara," is a simple octave *guajeo/montuno* performed by Juanito Márquez throughout the entire song. Play along with the track and then try to come up with another *guajeo/montuno* that works.

In order to execute *guajeos* and *montunos* on the guitar, one must first start from the example set by those pioneering guitarists within Latin jazz. Hopefully, the examples will show you how this is done. Then you can build upon these basic ideas and find your own way. As you will see in the next chapters, the application of *guajeos* and *montunos* on the guitar in a manner that is stylistically consistent is possible.

On the next page, I have included a chart which outlines my personal findings and observations regarding the various techniques used to adapt *guajeos* and *montunos* to the guitar. The chart shows an overview of the techniques used in each of the previous examples.

CHAPTER 2 — GUAJEOS AND MONTUNOS

Guajeo and Montuno Comparison Chart

Level of Difficulty	Technique	Pros/Cons
Easy to Medium	Single-note	• Easier to use • Does not produce a big sound since the guitar doesn't have string courses (pairs)
	String pairs	• Ease of use because it employs just the chord and combination of 1 & 3 or 2 & 4 strings
Medium to Difficult	Intervallic: octaves and compound intervals	• Difficult • Position changes • Tempo • Chord quality
	Intervallic: octave and single-note	• An adaptation that most resembles *tres* and piano • Requires technical facility • Upper structure harmonic reharmonization • Position changes
Difficult	Chords, triads, intervals and single-note	• An adaptation that marries *tres, cuatro* and piano with the guitar • Upper structure triad approach • String pairs • Intervals • Tension and release • Single-note • RH picking technique • LH technical issues • Tempo

*For technical ease, some guitarists tune their guitar in perfect 4ths to execute the *guajeos* and *montunos*. The tuning of fourths on guitar does indeed evoke the sonority of the *tres* and *cuatro*. However, at the time of this publication, there only exists one historical precedent that supports this possibility, when Bob Bianco used the fourth tuning with Eddie Palmieri on "Spiritual Indian." With the methods that I propose, the need for changing the tuning of the guitar is made obsolete.

CHAPTER 2   GUAJEOS AND MONTUNOS

Tres, Cuatro and *Requinto* Adaptations to the Guitar

From the *tres, cuatro, requinto* and the piano, we receive the valuable techniques of the *guajeo* and *montuno* that influence how guitarists adapt these patterns to their instrument. Although I encourage further study of these instruments, I understand that procuring these instruments is virtually impossible in some cases. However, the ability to play those instruments or simply listening to them will help you derive your conclusions about adaptations to the guitar. The following examples provide some valuable solutions that will help you to make these readaptations.

    The *tres* and the *cuatro* have double courses or string pairs, are higher-pitched, tuned differently, and have different scale lengths. I have come up with a step-by-step procedure to incorporate their sound and techniques to the guitar while also considering the piano's possibilities. Finally, a cross-examination is offered by comparing these adaptations to what previous guitarists had exhibited, as shown in the last chapter.

    The next example displays a single-note *guajeo* played by Niño Rivera on "Oye Mi Tres Montuno." The original *guajeo* is on the first staff of both examples. The second staff shows how the guitar harmonizes the original *guajeo* and adds an octave on the anticipations. When a *tres* is present, then this would be the best option, along with just strumming the chords as explained in the next chapter.

CHAPTER 2

GUAJEOS AND MONTUNOS

Track 293

CONTEMPORARY LATIN JAZZ GUITAR, VOL. 1

87

CHAPTER 2   *GUAJEOS* AND *MONTUNOS*

    However, another approach is on display in the example above. Look how the guitar maintains the original *montuno* in the beginning of bar 3 on beats 1 & 2, only to continue with a harmonization featuring 4ths and octaves. The next example below displays how a repetitive one-bar *montuno* pattern mixes with a two-bar *montuno* pattern.

CHAPTER 2

GUAJEOS AND *MONTUNOS*

Track 295

CONTEMPORARY LATIN JAZZ GUITAR, VOL. 1

89

CHAPTER 2 GUAJEOS AND MONTUNOS

Track 297

The example above displays alternating compound and closed interval *montunos* in the first staff, while the guitar is playing a traditional *tumbao* pattern over a traditional I-IV-V two-bar progression.

The following examples provide *guajeo* and *montuno* patterns over the three inversions of a C major triad. The execution of these exercises should be on strings 321 using pick and fingers or fingerstyle technique. The examples begin in root position while the *guajeo* uses octave and 3rds, then the 1st inversion using octave and 4ths, and finally the 2nd inversion using octave and 3rds again.

CHAPTER 2   *GUAJEOS* AND *MONTUNOS*

Track 299

Track 301

CONTEMPORARY LATIN JAZZ GUITAR, VOL. 1   91

CHAPTER 2 — GUAJEOS AND MONTUNOS

Track 303

The next set of examples display *guajeos* and *montunos* for the same C maj triad that use different interval combinations. The first example uses parallel 6ths, the second uses 5ths and 6ths, and third uses 6ths and 5ths.

Track 305

CHAPTER 2   GUAJEOS AND MONTUNOS

Track 307

Track 309

The next example, a chordal *montuno* with inversions of the triad, demonstrates how one can divide the chord voicing among the rhythmic pattern. Notice how the Cmaj7 drop-two voicing on beat 1 alternates with its inner E minor triad. This is one of the most

CHAPTER 2 GUAJEOS AND MONTUNOS

convenient ways of playing *guajeos* and *montunos* on guitar: by utilizing string groups of the existing voicing.

Track 311 Chordal *Montuno* with Inversion of Triad (Drop-Two to Drop-Three Voicings)

In the example above, a drop-two voicing of Cmaj7 is C G B E. This voicing is on the 5432 strings. When the 5th is doubled in the voicing, the G or 5th is on the 1st string. The E minor triad, which is needed for the voicing and rhythmic pattern execution, is conveniently located on strings 432. Because we would use the claw technique to execute our *guajeos* and *montunos*, our *medio* (middle), *anillo* (ring) and (*meñique*) little finger of the right hand are conveniently situated to grab the triad.

The pick will concentrate on playing the lowest note of the voicing. Because of the convenience of the voicing and correct position, executing *guajeos* and *montunos* in this manner is the easiest and quickest form of delivering results when pressed to play a Latin song without previous knowledge of the style.

CHAPTER 2   *GUAJEOS* AND *MONTUNOS*

In the next example below, we will observe Yomo Toro on "La Pepita de Mango" and a possible guitar adaptation. The first staff features the original line as played by Yomo Toro. The second staff features the guitar adaptation showing the note analysis in two lines. The top line analysis is for the top note, and the second line is for the bottom note. This type of analysis brings out the importance of note choice so that you can adapt this to your playing situation. Once this is understood, then you can use a more convenient form of interval analysis.

Each four-bar phrase shows yet another variation of the original *guajeo/montuno* that Yomo plays. The guitar adaptation serves two functions: to support the original *cuatro* part and also substitute for it.

CHAPTER 2 — GUAJEOS AND MONTUNOS

Track 313

Suggested Fingerings found on page 8

CHAPTER 2

GUAJEOS AND MONTUNOS

CONTEMPORARY LATIN JAZZ GUITAR, VOL. 1

CHAPTER 2   *GUAJEOS* AND *MONTUNOS*

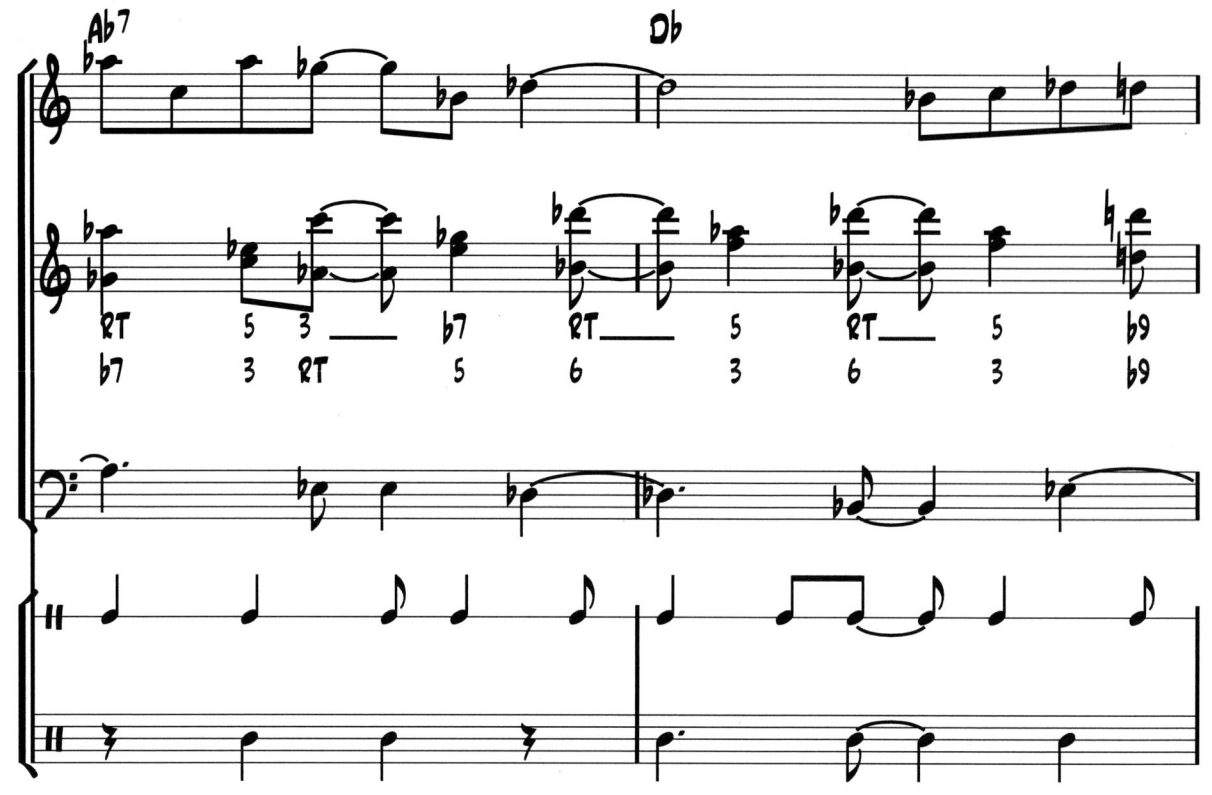

98   CONTEMPORARY LATIN JAZZ GUITAR, VOL. 1

CHAPTER 2   GUAJEOS AND MONTUNOS

The *requinto* offers high-pitched melodic ideas with a more Latin style of the bebop scale. The *requinto's* size and timbre give a more beautiful sound in the same high, melodic range instead of the guitar. This is easily executed on the guitar by playing on the upper two strings and playing above the IX/X fret and beyond. The example below displays an introduction played on *requinto* by El Güero Gil. The introduction features diatonic sequences, chromatic passing tones and approaches in an arpeggiated and scalar methodology. This is easily executable on the guitar.

In the next example, Los Guaracheros de Oriente demonstrates intervallic ideas in bar 3-6. Notice how the *requinto* is alternating between intervals of 3rds, 6ths, tritone and single-note lines that clearly outline the dominant chord quality of D7. This example also demonstrates how the *requinto* part blends with the *guajeo* of the guitarist.

CONTEMPORARY LATIN JAZZ GUITAR, VOL. 1

CHAPTER 2

GUAJEOS AND MONTUNOS

CHAPTER 2 — *GUAJEOS* AND *MONTUNOS*

Requinto (top line) and guitar (bottom line)

In the transcription above of "Frutas del Caney" by Los Guaracheros de Oriente, we have an eleven-bar introduction where the *requinto* begins with a pickup note into the song. The guitar displays the traditional role of accompanist, playing guitar *tumbao* with harmonic and bass support. One can specifically see how the *requinto* played the melody and how the accompanying guitar *tumbao* relates to it.

The simplest way to add more "Latin-sounding" melodic elements to your improvisations is to adapt *requinto* harmonic minor/chromatic-flavored, single-note lines in the upper register, intervallic (3rds) ideas, and increased speed to your playing. In conclusion, play through the examples and try to apply these patterns and ideas to other songs or progressions that you enjoy.

The *tres, cuatro* and *requinto* all have rich and distinct musical traditions. For the purposes of this book, I have brought up some of the many techniques that might be applied to the guitar.

Piano Adaptations and Solutions for the Guitar

It is impossible to discuss Latin jazz guitar without even mentioning or contemplating the influence of the role of the piano. Most guitarists believe that one must apply and imitate the piano's readaptations of *guajeo* and *montuno* (which originated on the *tres, cuatro, and requinto)* to the guitar. Although that might be true to some degree, much of what is played on piano cannot be reproduced on the guitar for sonic and technical reasons.

CHAPTER 2　　GUAJEOS AND MONTUNOS

Track 315　　*Suggested Fingerings found on page 5*

CONTEMPORARY LATIN JAZZ GUITAR, VOL. 1

CHAPTER 2   GUAJEOS AND MONTUNOS

This above example is a typical *montuno* in the style of what pianist Gilberto "El Pulpo" Colón Jr. plays with Giovanni Hidalgo on a Latin Percussion video jam. The top line features a simplified piano *montuno*, while the second line offers a guitar adaptation that doesn't clash with the pianist.

Track 317

The example above shows how a typical *descarga* piano part in the style of Bebo Valdés is adapted for the guitar. The adaptation features chord voicings that are arpeggiated, along with the use of octaves and 2nds. Notice also how the chord voicings are sustained too. The artist transcription on pages 110-111 features the guitar part of Edgardo Miranda combined with the piano adaptation on the original recording so that you can hear how both parts interact with each other.

CHAPTER 2 GUAJEOS AND MONTUNOS

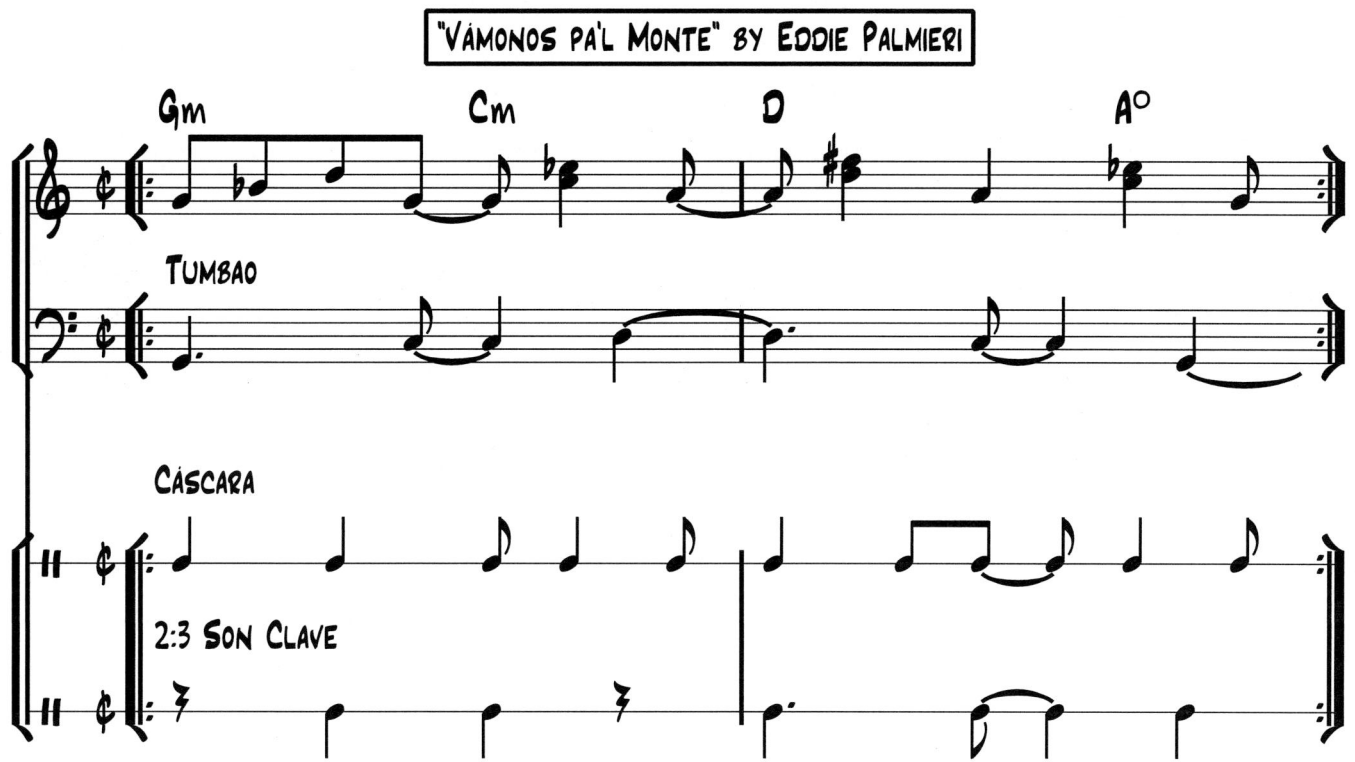

Track 319

CONTEMPORARY LATIN JAZZ GUITAR, VOL. 1

CHAPTER 2   GUAJEOS AND MONTUNOS

The example above shows the iconic *montuno* on "Vámonos pa'l Monte" by Eddie Palmieri, while Track 319 shows a typical minor 4 bar vamp using the same progression. However, bar 3 stays on the D7 and bar 4 resolves to the Gmin and Cmin. Both of these iconic *montunos* fit particularly well because of their usage of triads that have logical fingerings on the guitar.

Track 321

Suggested Strings: 432
Suggested Fingerings found on page 7

CHAPTER 2   *GUAJEOS* AND *MONTUNOS*

Track 323   *Suggested Fingerings found on page 7*

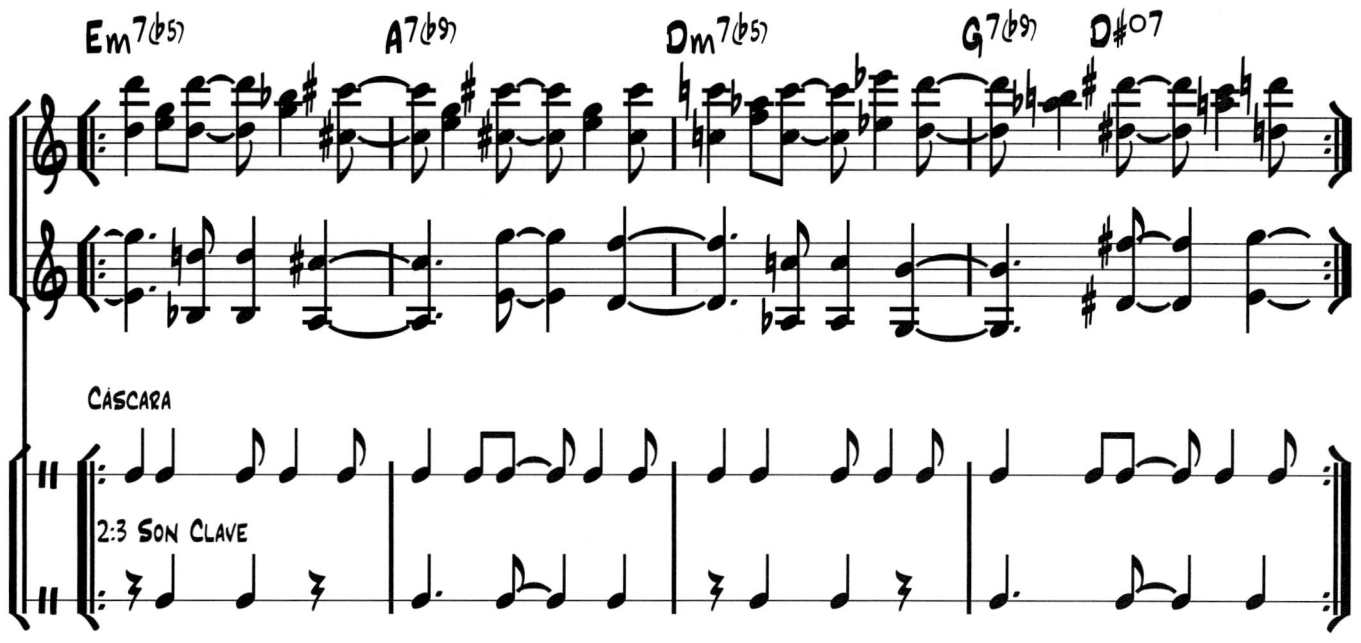

The previous examples show how a guitarist can play pianistic *montunos* while another guitarist plays tenths. In this case, two guitarists can simulate what one pianist plays but with our own unique sound.

The example above is the iconic "Morning" piano *montuno* pattern over a cha-cha-chá. This pattern is easily executable on strings 432. However, one must pay close attention to having the correct three-note voicings that maintain the harmonic quality of each chord. Not only that, but it must also be comfortable to play on the guitar too. Try to play along with the original recording.

The solutions I have laid forth for you were born from that unique and formidable readaptation of *tres guajeos* to the piano. However, with these new variations (in fingerings, voicings and harmonic considerations), I provide you with the necessary tools to make credible guitar reductions/readaptations of your favorite Latin pianist's *montunos*.

How to Interact with the Pianist

In order to accurately understand why a guitarist played a certain way, we need to first assess the function of the guitar as three distinct parts: soloist, ensemble and rhythm section. If you look at any YouTube video or any recording, these aspects may or may not come to the foreground. So, what do these parts really entail?

The soloist covers the interpretation of melodies and solos while reverting to an ensemble and rhythm section role during the duration of the song. The ensemble part depicts the guitarist as another instrument, doubling horn lines and interludes (*moñas*). Finally, the rhythm section role puts the guitarist in their natural habitat, playing right-hand rhythmic variation patterns of the *clave, cáscara, tumbao* and percussion with occasional doublings of the piano *montuno*.

The most classic portrayal of a guitarist covering all of these roles alongside a pianist can be found with guitarist Juanito Márquez and pianist Felipe Dulzaides, Irakere guitarist Carlos Emilio Morales and pianist Chucho Valdés, Edgardo Miranda and pianist Bebo Valdés, and Kenny Burrell with Cal Tjader, to name a few.

CHAPTER 2 GUAJEOS AND MONTUNOS

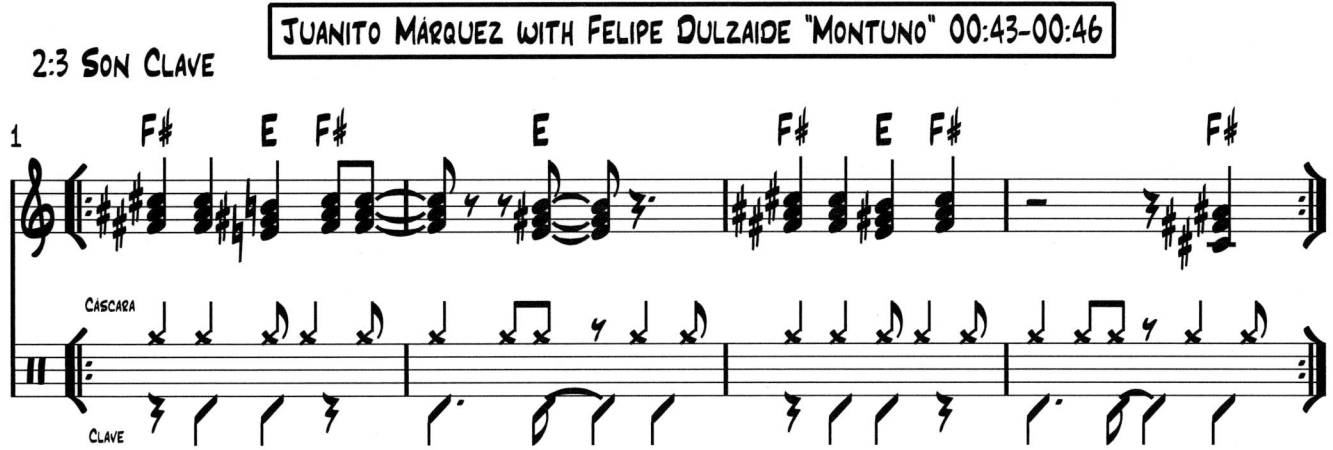

"Montuno" by Cachaíto featuring Felipe Dulzaides (piano) and Juanito Marquez (guitar). On this recording, we have an arranged part that features the guitar playing sparse rhythmic figures, varying registers, and unison figures with the piano.

CONTEMPORARY LATIN JAZZ GUITAR, VOL. 1

CHAPTER 2 — GUAJEOS AND MONTUNOS

CHAPTER 2 GUAJEOS AND MONTUNOS

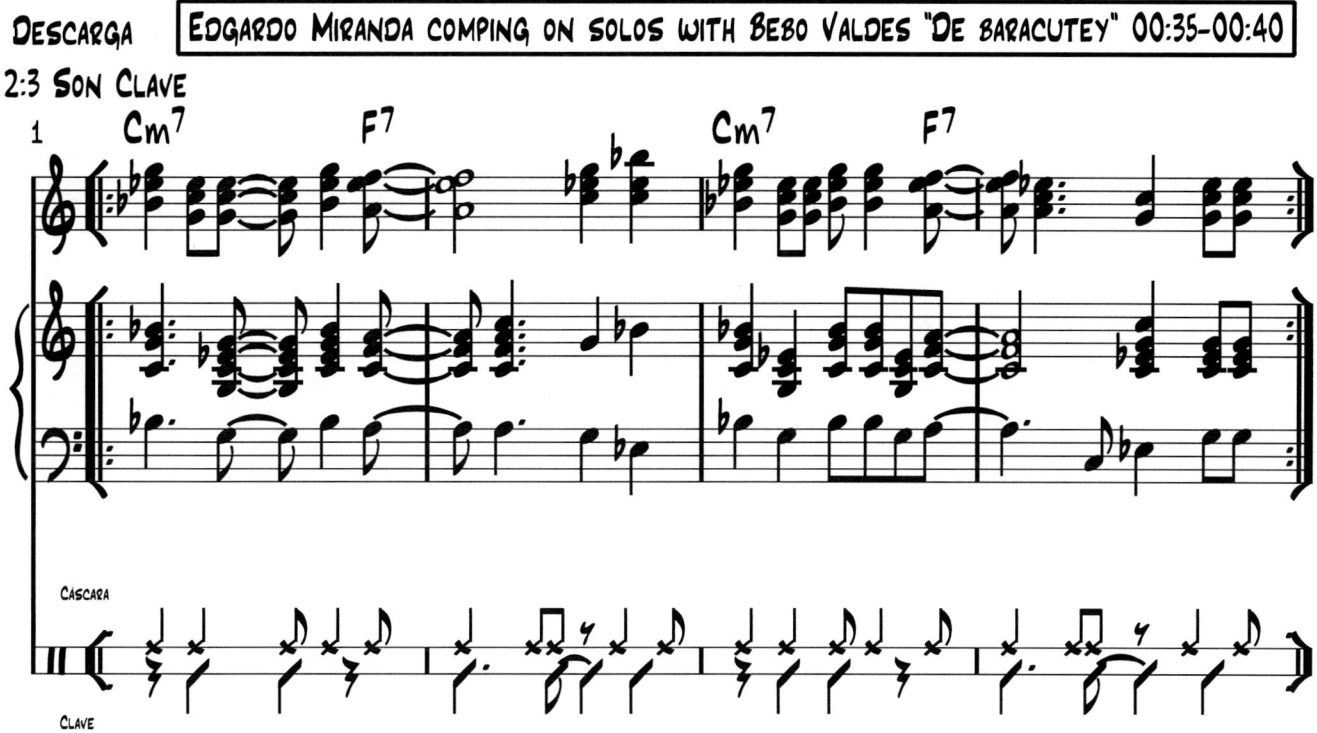

In the examples above, Edgardo Miranda is playing on a *descarga* in the middle and upper register, while Bebo Valdés supports the bass and plays in the middle register.

During the solo section, we have a classic *descarga* comping situation where we can hear how Edgardo and Bebo blend together simultaneously on a *montuno*. This short example shows how they exploited range, triadic voicings and rhythmic space. One can derive one bar motives from the recording for your own purposes. Previously in example Track 317, I have taken some of those ideas from the solo section as an exercise.

The following examples display how Clare Fischer utilizes the guitar in his compositions as an ensemble instrument.

CHAPTER 2 GUAJEOS AND MONTUNOS

The above example shows how Clare used the guitar to play the lower line and to double the chord voicings. In this two-bar vamp, a B♭/C tonality is established while using typical Fischer-esque voicings and counterpoint that resolves to a three-note voicing.

CHAPTER 2 GUAJEOS AND MONTUNOS

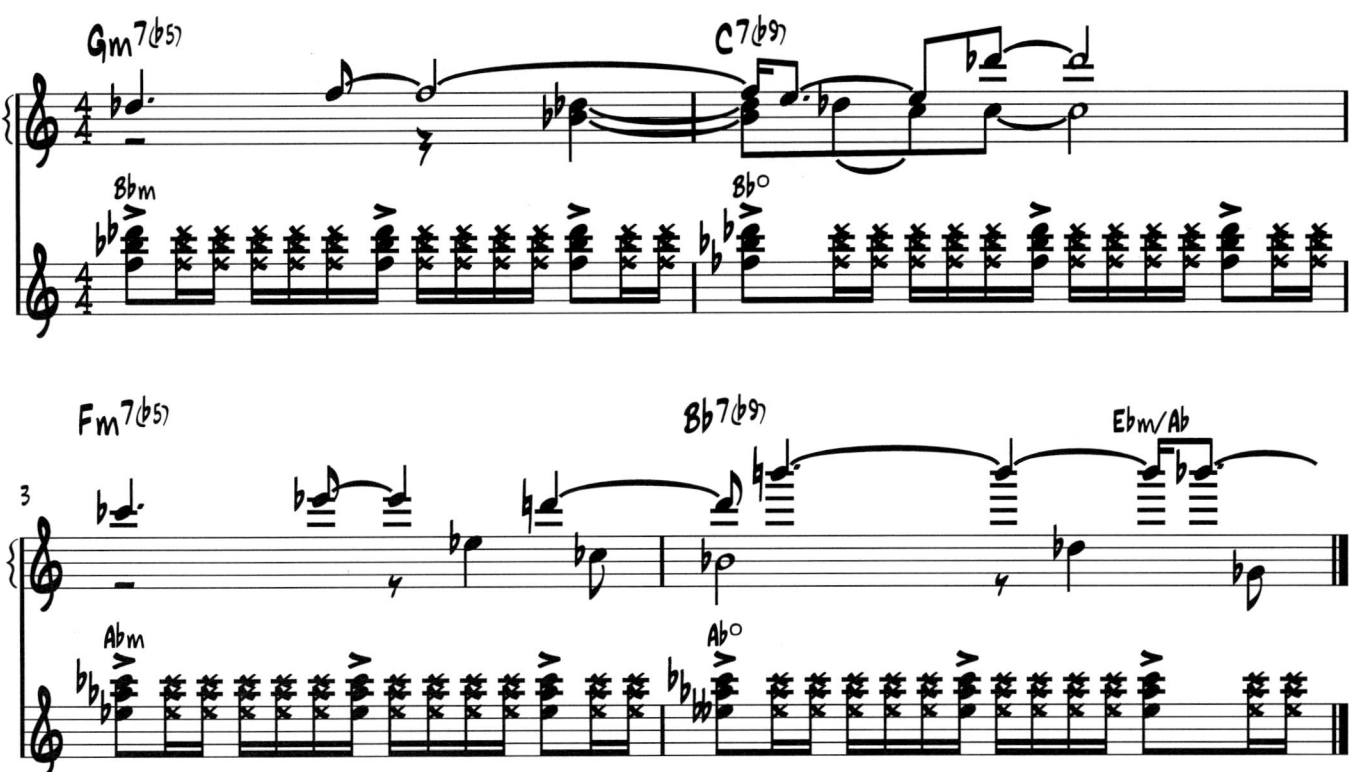

The above example now shows Rick Zunigar playing specifically written upper-structure voicings that blend well behind Clare's solo. This example also demonstrates Fischer's concept of arranging guitar voicings as an extension of his left hand.

CHAPTER 2   *GUAJEOS* AND *MONTUNOS*

CHA-CHA-CHÁ
2:3 SON CLAVE — CLARE FISCHER'S ARRANGED GUITAR GUAJEO PLAYED BY DANNY EMBREY ON "PAVILLÓN"

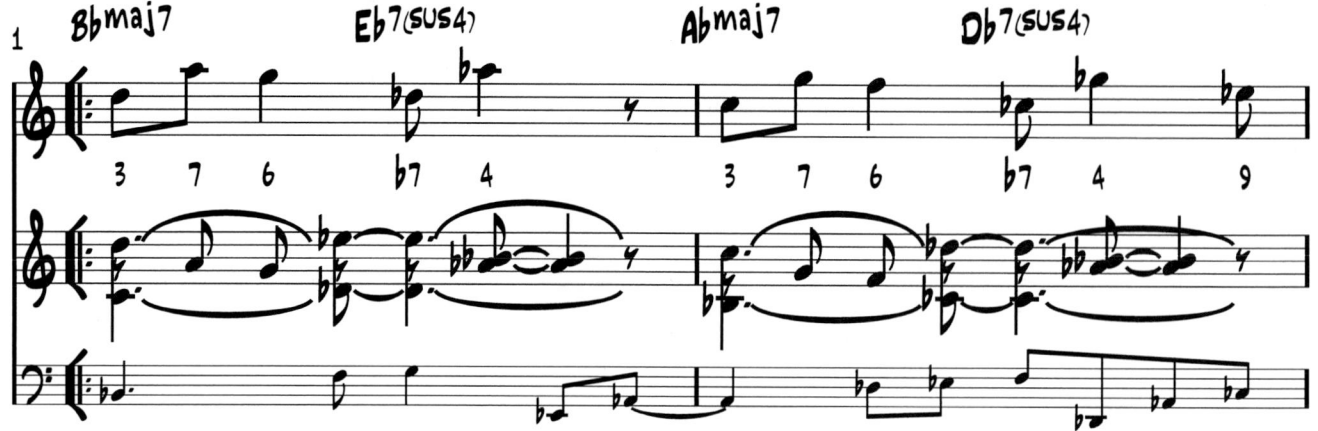

The two examples above display how Clare Fischer used the guitar as an ensemble instrument, played by Danny Embrey on "Pavillón." In the top example, the guitar is playing fourth voicings in a rhythmic pattern while a percussion solo is underway. In the lower example, the guitar on the 1st line and the piano on the 2nd line exhibit yet another brilliantly harmonized *guajeo/montuno* counterpoint in 2:3 *son clave*.

CHAPTER 2 GUAJEOS AND MONTUNOS

The example above shows how Edgardo Miranda plays three-note voicings that support the key rhythm of *danzón* and good register choice that allows for the guitar to cohabit the space with Bebo Valdés' piano playing.

The piano's influence on the guitar's process of readapting *tres* and *cuatro* parts is a very profound subject that warrants extra careful attention to voicings and register. In Steve Khan's opinion, "the harmonic language of Latin jazz changed dramatically when Eddie Palmieri and Chick Corea came on the scene with their use of more modern jazz harmony."[4]

The *tres, cuatro, requinto* and piano, each with their own unique characteristics, offer a wide array of techniques for the electric guitar to creatively build upon. Some might evaluate this as mere imitation. However, through the guitar's filtration of those techniques, this process created a unique voice that is the electric guitar in Latin jazz.

In certain situations, there are clear limitations to the guitar's role due to technical and sonic constraints. These technical restraints are unique to the guitar because of the guitar's tuning, the scale length, the model of the specific instrument, and sonic qualities. There could also even be highly individualistic restraints that require more technical facilities to execute them. Perhaps these are the same reasons why Arsenio Rodríguez replaced the gui-

---

4 Steve Khan, interview by Neff Irizarry II. (December 19, 2019).

CHAPTER 2   *GUAJEOS* AND *MONTUNOS*

tar with the piano, thus sealing the guitar's fate in history. Because of this, the guitar player needs to use an innovative approach to guitar-specific technical devices such as intervals, different string groupings, and chord inversions that would offer a different sonic texture.

The innovative approach I have presented gives unique insight into the possible usage of combinations of single-note, double stop, and three or more note voicings within the *guajeo*. This usage creates a sound unique only to the electric guitar, which offers an alternative that is more than just a pure imitation of the *tres*, *cuatro*, *requinto*, and piano. It IS the contemporary Latin jazz guitar.

CHAPTER 3
Left & Right Hand Technique for *Guajeos/Montunos*

The new concepts that I have created are formulated and derived from standard guitar technique and the readaptation of more traditional string instruments and idiomatic piano devices to the guitar.

Compared to the double string courses prominent to chordophones in the style, the very nature of the guitar's tuning and single-string characteristics makes it almost impossible to directly copy techniques from folkloric instruments such as the Cuban *tres* and the Puerto Rican *cuatro*. To establish a more guitar-congruent adaptation, I have created a two-pronged strategy focusing on the left hand and the right hand.

The implementation of the left-hand technique of consecutive octaves, a standard jazz guitar technique pioneered by Wes Montgomery, is used to imitate those instruments' double-coursed sound on the top three or four strings. However, the tempo, chord progressions and chord voicings offer distinct challenges that execution with octaves alone couldn't solve. So, I devised a set of alternative techniques as well.

The first combination is achieved through a series of octaves and intervals, as demonstrated in the following example.

Track 325 2:3 *Son Clave Guajeo* *Suggested Fingerings found on pages 91–94*

CHAPTER 3 LEFT & RIGHT HAND TECHNIQUE FOR *GUAJEOS/MONTUNOS*

The second combination conveniently uses string pairs 1 & 3 and 2 & 4 or any non-consecutive string grouping on any drop-two chord voicing, which enabled harmonic clarity and rhythmic proficiency to execute the typical idiomatic devices of *guajeos* and *montunos*.

Track 327 *2:3 Son Clave Guajeo*   *Suggested Fingerings found on pages 91–94*

While some guitarists use only the classical fingerstyle technique of PIMA and its accompanying strumming technique (*rasgueo*, etc.), I favor using the hybrid method of pick and fingers or the claw and pick strumming.

Tracks 325 & 327 are executed using pick *medio (middle)* or pick and *anillo (ring)*. Track 325 uses pick and *medio (middle)* for the octave and then only pick on the single notes. Track 327 alternates between pick *medio (middle)* and pick *anillo (ring)*.

- When executing *guajeos/montunos* that use octaves or smaller intervals, one should use the pick and *medio (middle)*.

- When executing *guajeos/montunos* that use intervals greater than an octave, use the pick and *anillo (ring)*.

This technique allows the guitarist to alternate between pick and *medio (middle)* and pick and *anillo (ring)* to facilitate fast and articulate movements, emphasizing the rhythmic and harmonic characteristics conducive to the style. Combining these new left-hand and right-hand techniques allows the guitarist to execute the necessary *guajeos* and *montunos* with ease.

In order to enable these techniques, it is important to use substitutions based upon triadic, upper structure and intervallic devices that provide harmonic clarity for adapting Latin pianistic devices to the instrument. Since the *guajeos* and *montunos* on the guitar are executed on the top three strings (321) and piano voicings are frequently three or more

CHAPTER 3 — LEFT & RIGHT HAND TECHNIQUE FOR *GUAJEOS/MONTUNOS*

notes per voicing, I divided the harmonic structures into three-note groups that provided maximum harmonic clarity.

For instance, Fmin7 contains F A♭ C E♭, but for executing a *montuno*, I would play an A♭ triad (A♭ C E♭). If the chord is Fmin7(9), then I would play a *guajeo* that sometimes utilized two triads such as A♭ triad and C minor triad.

Track 329 *Suggested Fingerings found on pages 91–94*

2:3 SON CLAVE

Track 331 *Suggested Fingerings found on pages 91–94*

2:3 SON CLAVE

Disclaimer: I included this section in the book because it recommends guitar-specific techniques for you to consider when executing the etudes. These are techniques that I found useful, but please try to find technical solutions that work for your own unique way of playing. *Please don't injure yourself in the playing process.*

CHAPTER 4
Traditional Styles

In the traditional styles of Latin music, the guitar's function is to support the melodic, harmonic, bass movement and rhythmic aspects of the music. Naturally, depending upon the style and instrumentation, the guitar covers all three functions or one of those functions at a time. These functions are traditionally on display with the interplay between traditional instruments and the piano in Latin music.

In a solo or duo function, the guitar covers all of those aspects, as in the case of the music of Ñico Rojas or the guitarists of the "Filin" movement, such as Juanito Márquez, Pablo Cano and Froilán Amézaga, for instance. In this solo or duo function, the guitar repertoire of the period is influenced by three sources: classical[1], folkloric styles, and jazz.

The next example below shows the jazz influence on Afro-Cuban guitar. Pablo Cano's guitar introduction is very consistent with what many bebop guitarists played during the time period.

---

1 Due to the scope of this book, please refer to the selected discography and the wealth of nationalistic classical music tradition of Latin America. One might begin with Ñico Rojas, Guyan and Leo Brouwer.

CHAPTER 4   TRADITIONAL STYLES

From the interaction between *tres* and guitar and *requinto* and guitar, we gain two important insights into the rhythmic support and the arrangement or orchestration that allowed these two instruments to coexist in the same musical space. They are the rhythmic strumming pattern and the guitar tumbao with bass and harmonic support.

These two insights also influenced the piano. However, the strumming sound of the right hand of the guitar cannot be easily reproduced on piano, since it is unique to string instruments.

When we get to the Cuban *son* and, most notably, Arsenio Rodríguez's band, we no longer have the guitar covering bass movement, but rather the harmonic and rhythmic functions. This period came to affect the guitar's role the most by providing a rhythmic foundation that brought about other imitations and variations of the percussion rhythms, such as the *marcha* (the main pattern) of the conga, the cowbell pattern, the *cáscara* of the *timbales,* or the patterns of the *batá* drums.

There were many early guitarists who pioneered the right-hand technique, but the most recorded is Marcelino Guerra with Arsenio Rodríguez. He would go on to influence his contemporaries such as Juanito Márquez and the next generation of guitarists such as Carlos Emilio "El Gordo" Morales, Kiko Cubano, Pablo Menéndez, Carlos Santana and Edgardo Miranda, to name a few.

In the trio format of Los Panchos and Los Guaracheros de Oriente, the guitar supported the vocalists with harmonic, rhythmic and bass movement while the *requinto* covered the melodies.

CHAPTER 4 — TRADITIONAL STYLES

CHAPTER 4 — TRADITIONAL STYLES

Guitarists tend to play right-hand strumming patterns when traditional instruments or the piano are featured. The guitar's role is then akin to a rhythm section instrument, reinforcing the conga's rhythmic patterns, or the *clave*, *cáscara* and *tumbao*. The examples on the next page display these properties.

Track 333

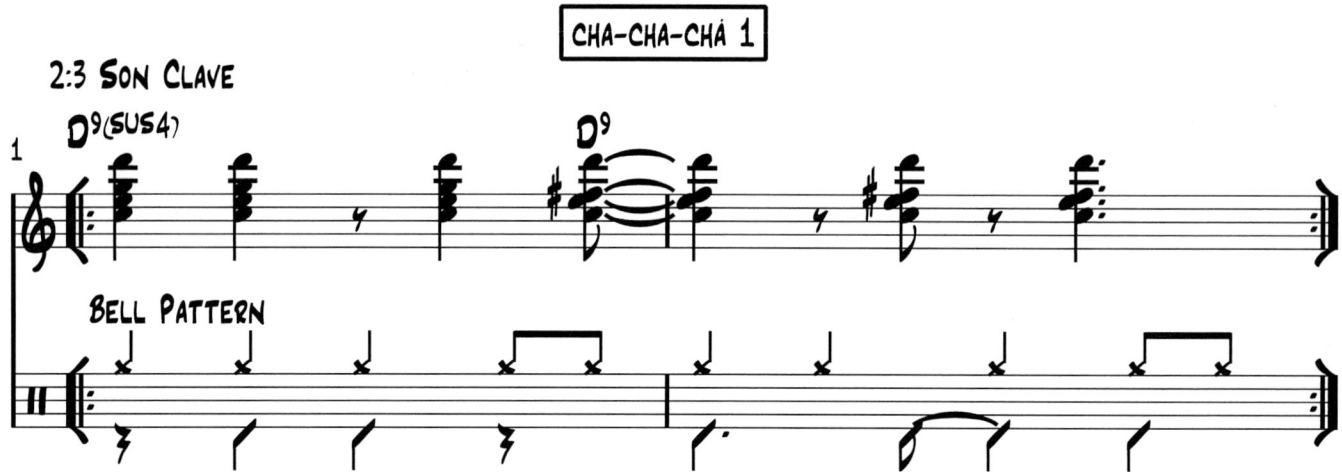

Track 335

CHAPTER 4   TRADITIONAL STYLES

CHA-CHA-CHÁ
2:3 Son Clave

CHA-CHA-CHÁ
2:3 Son Clave

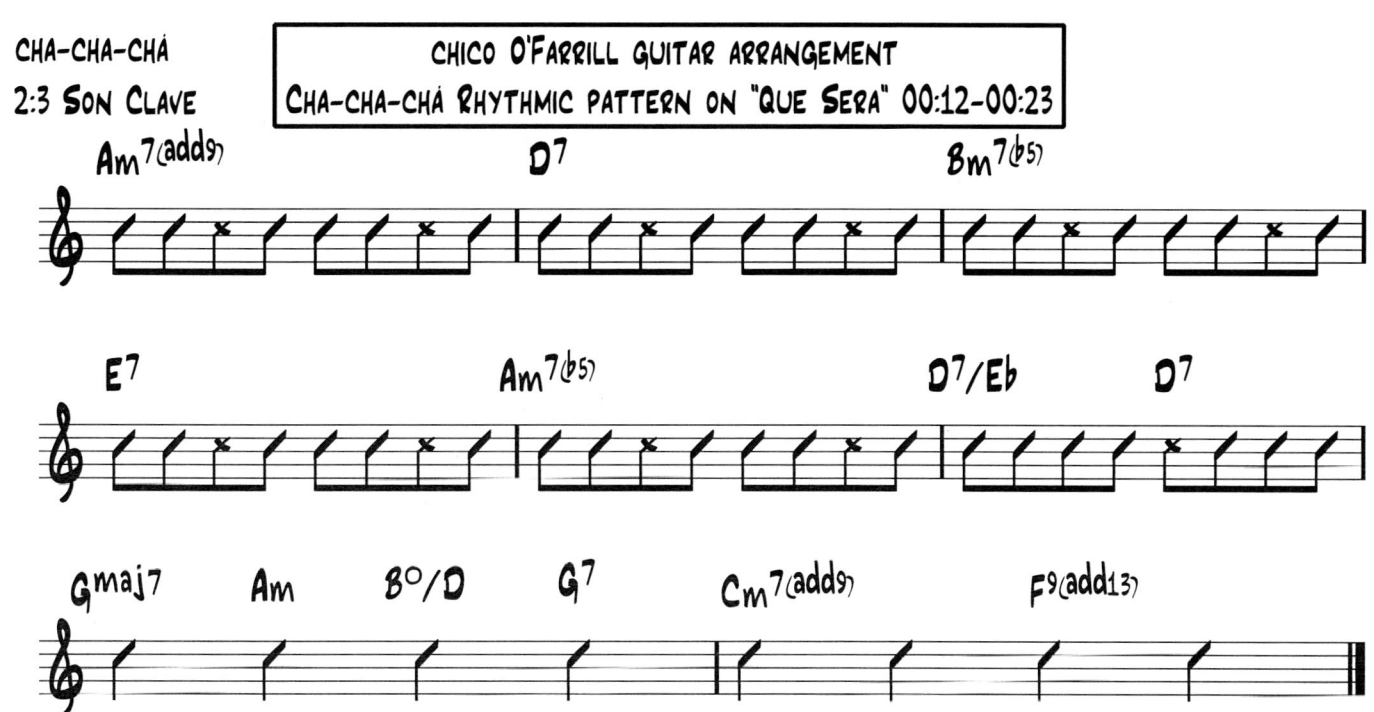

CONTEMPORARY LATIN JAZZ GUITAR, VOL. 1

CHAPTER 4 — TRADITIONAL STYLES

126 — CONTEMPORARY LATIN JAZZ GUITAR, VOL. 1

CHAPTER 4

TRADITIONAL STYLES

GUAJIRA
2:3 Son Clave

"El vaiven de mi carreta" Los Guaracheros de Oriente

GUAJIRA
2:3 Son Clave

"Sopa de Pichón" Son de Clave de Oro

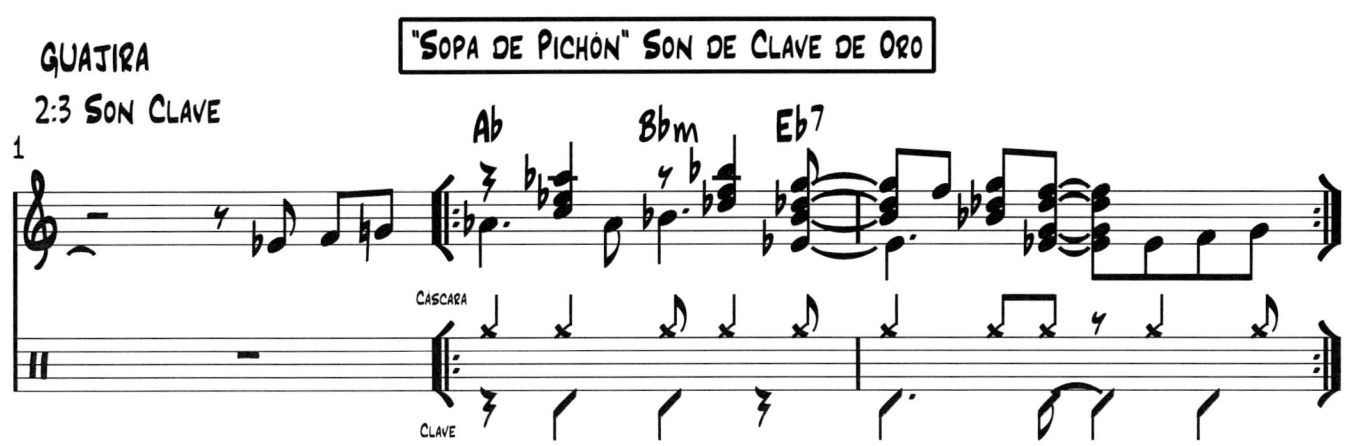

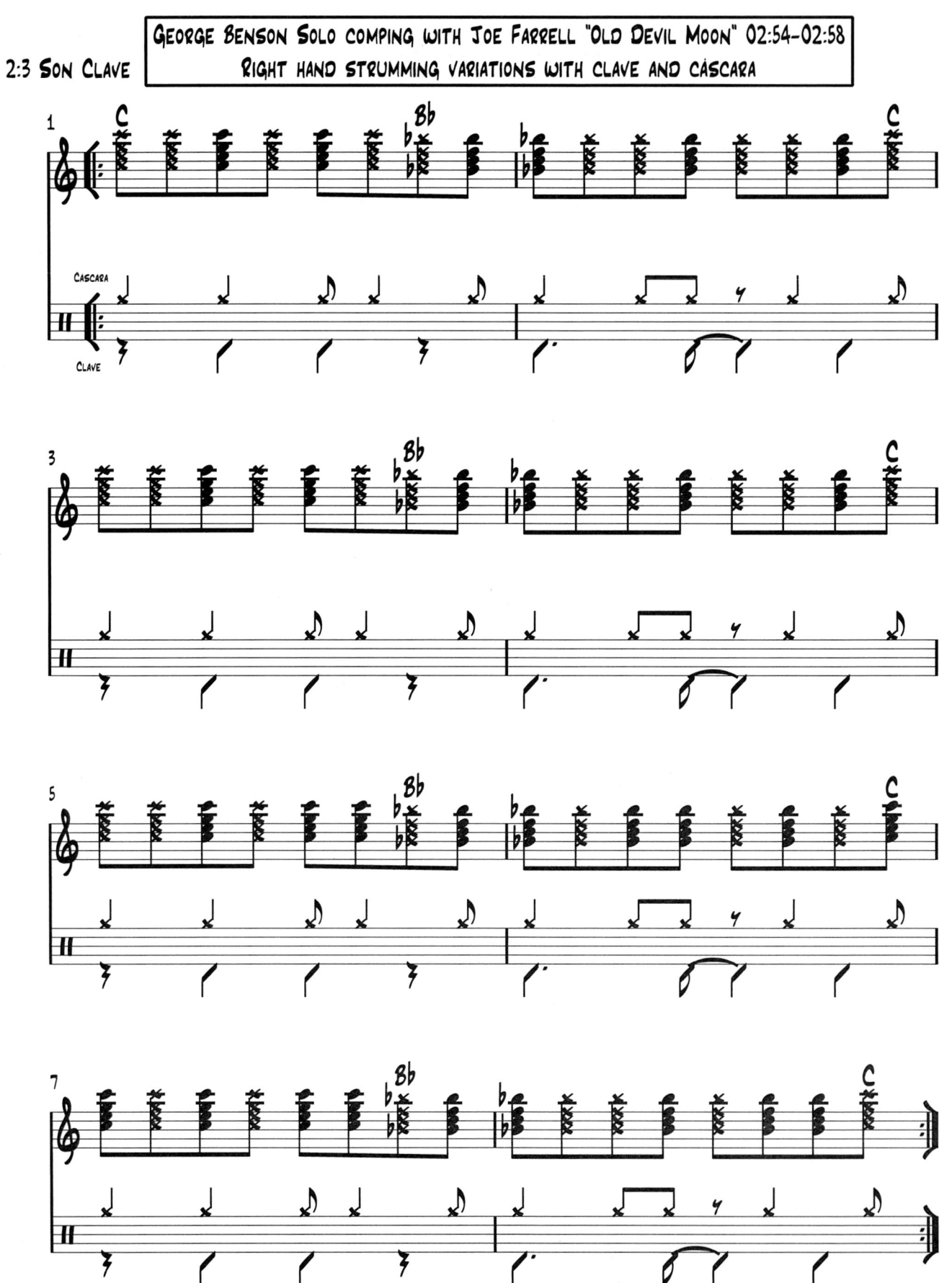

CHAPTER 5
Influential Guitarists

Without the inventiveness and forward-thinking of guitarists, arrangers and composers that made the electric guitar work in an Afro-Cuban, Latin jazz format, we wouldn't have had an example to be inspired by or to build upon.

Legendary bandleaders such as Tito Puente, Chico O'Farrill, Willie Bobo, Cal Tjader, Ray Mantilla, Clare Fischer, Paul Alicea and Eddie Palmieri featured guitar in their bands and recordings. Many guitarists found work in Latin jazz, but few recordings document their exploits as a soloist and leader.

The eight most influential guitarists in Latin jazz featuring electric guitar are: Juanito "El Maestro" Márquez, Paul "Payo" Alicea, Sonny Henry, Edgardo Miranda, Carlos Emilio "El Gordo" Morales, Bobby Redfield, Carlos Santana, and Steve Khan.

I have chosen these guitarists because of the overwhelming evidence that confirms their contributions to the style. However, I have listed many other guitarists that have delved into the style in the anthology of influential guitarists in Latin jazz on page 191.

The musicians' creative nature and the cultural environment they found themselves in provided fertile ground that increased demand from the public, while influencing fellow musicians. The guitarists Juanito "El Maestro" Márquez and his counterpart, Paul Alicea, were famous during the mambo craze of the 1950s; their concept of how to feature the guitar within the genre helped to establish a precedent for the next wave of guitarists in the 1960's that would apply the "Latin" sounds to jazz. The application is most visible with such jazz guitarists as Sonny Henry, Barney Kessel, Grant Green, Attila Zoller, Kenny Burrell and George Benson, who were, in fact, their contemporaries.

CHAPTER 5 — INFLUENTIAL GUITARISTS

Each player employed different tactics for the best application of Afro-Cuban & Latin jazz guitar to their situation. For some, it was just a matter of reading a composed part, and for others it was more of a natural talent related to their culture or exposure to Latin music. Chapters 5 and 6 give a brief idea on the chordal and improvisational aspects of these guitarists. This information will also be the subject of Volume 2 of this book, which will show how harmonic minor, tonal bop-based and pentatonic-style improvisation define the contemporary Latin jazz guitar.

Here are some of the most influential guitarists that shaped the electric guitar's role in Afro-Cuban & Latin jazz.

Juanito "El Maestro" Márquez

Cuban guitarist, composer and arranger, Juanito "El Maestro" Márquez' influence on Latin music and the Latin guitar spans four decades. His talents are on display within this book as well as in the timeline located at the end of the book. However, by combining jazz guitar vocabulary with the Afro-Cuban traditional styles, "El Maestro" revolutionized the use of the guitar (both with and without traditional instruments), and has laid a foundation for other guitarists to emulate. His recordings as a leader, such as *Juanito Marquez y su Combo, Arrímate pa'cá*, and as a sideman with Felipe Dulzaides, exemplify the early role of Latin jazz guitar.

Paul "Payo" Alicea

The guitarist and founder of La Playa Sextet, Paul Alicea was an important figure in the development of the role of the guitar in Latin jazz. Paul's recordings with La Playa Sextet from 1955–1979 are a valuable source for the modern guitarist to learn about the role of the electric guitar in Latin jazz. It is important to note that Paul's sideman and second guitarist, Francisco "Frankie" Sánchez (La Plata Sextette) was also instrumental in the development of Latin jazz guitar. He broke away from La Playa Sextet to form the rival group La Plata Sextette. According to Bobby Sanabria,

> I believe that Paul's innovation was because nobody was gonna hire him really unless he formed his own band, so the 2nd guitar would fulfill the role of like what a piano player would do. Just like in Cuban *conjuntos* during the time of

Arsenio (Rodríguez) you have the guitarist doing what they called *capetillo* then the *tresero* is doing *guajeos*, arpeggiating the chords. The same thing with Paul—that was his innovation. The other thing, his was the only group doing that besides the Plata Sextette. Other than those two groups… There weren't any other groups."[1]

Paul's *guajeo* adaptations to the guitar have been transcribed and featured in this book. However, his *guajeo*, chordal and improvisational skills are best displayed on the song "Baila Ramón"[2] from the recording *Pachanga with La Playa Sextet*.

Sonny Henry

Clarence "Sonny" Henry was a jazz guitarist and composer, best known for his song "Evil Ways" made famous by Carlos Santana. Besides composing "Evil Ways," Sonny was instrumental in establishing the role of electric guitar in Latin jazz during the 1960's with Willie Bobo's group. Songs such as "Sham Time"[3] and "It's Not Unusual,"[4] among others, feature Sonny's guitar *guajeos* and *montunos* with Bobo. His adaptations of *guajeos* and *montunos* are an invaluable source for the guitarist and have been featured as part of this book. More information regarding selected recordings that show his guitar adaptations can be found in the Timeline of Selected Recordings Section.

Edgardo Miranda

Edgardo Miranda is a mild-mannered Puerto Rican guitarist who bridged Puerto Rican traditional guitar influences with jazz. His contribution to establishing the role of electric guitar in Latin jazz is well-documented in his work with Tito Puente, Jerry Gonzalez, Rafael Cortijo, Daniel Ponce, and on the musical soundtrack "Capeman." According to Bobby Sanabria's first-hand account:

---

1 Bobby Sanabria, interview by Neff Irizarry II. *The Role of the guitar in Latin Jazz* (April 3, 2020).

2 La Playa Sextet, "La Playa Sextette - Baila con Ramon" posted by Cesar Bernal Aguilar Aug 3, 2017, YouTube Video, 3:12, https://www.youtube.com/watch?v=w2htqGPm4fs.

3 Willie Bobo, "Willie Bobo - Sham Time," posted by 45's, Mar 31, 2018, YouTube Video, 5:45, https://www.youtube.com/watch?v=1dAxDWRLnO0.

4 Willie Bobo, "Willie Bobo – It's not unusual," posted by 1951Fidel, Sep 28, 2012, YouTube Video, 2:19, https://www.youtube.com/watch?v=8GdyKMh_9Fg.

Edgardo is the connection between the adaptation of the folkloric vocabulary of the tres, cuatro and the guitar to the electric guitar in jazz. He knew how to play all the chordophone instruments such as cuatro, tres, laúd, tiple, banjo and cavaquinho. Some musicians are conscious of the clave but it's entirely a different subject for them to intuitively play in clave with a sense of freedom. Edgardo was one of those musicians that had the clave in his DNA, that clave wise. If you transcribe his solos, you would see the fluidity of his phrases in clave. His solos are beautiful examples of how to solo in clave with a harmonic approach consistent with Jazz."[5]

His improvisational skills display a strong bebop, Afro-Cuban, and Puerto Rican traditional vocabulary while adhering to the Afro-Cuban rhythmic structure. A brilliant example of this is on Bebo Valdés' "Ecuacion"[6] and Bobby Sanabria's version of the Joe Henderson classic, "Caribbean Fire Dance."[7]

Carlos Emilio "El Gordo" Morales

Cuban guitarist Carlos Emilio Morales was a founding member of the group Irakere and considered a key figure in the development of Afro-Cuban jazz. He is also credited with being the link between Afro-Cuban music and jazz guitar.

Carlos' early influences draw from the Mexican trio format with such artists as Los Panchos and Trio Matamoros, jazz guitarists such as Barney Kessel and Tal Farlow, as well as Cuban guitarist Pablo Cano. His influences reflect the same conclusions that the author has established throughout this book, putting a high importance on understanding the full scope of Latin music's past and its link to Latin jazz.

---

5 Bobby Sanabria, interview by Neff Irizarry II. *The Role of the guitar in Latin Jazz* (April 3, 2020).

6 Bebo Valdés, "Bebo Valdes-Ecuación," posted by Joseito 12, July 15, 2018, YouTube Video, 11:37, https://www.youtube.com/watch?v=NqZrz3qehHA.

7 Bobby Sanabria y Ascensión, "Bobby Sanabria y Ascensión- Caribbean Fire Dance," posted by Universal Music Group, Dec 27, 2018, YouTube Video, 7:28, https://www.youtube.com/watch?v=m0NTc5H82xM.

CHAPTER 5   INFLUENTIAL GUITARISTS

Carlos echoes the same sentiment of Clare Fischer's ideal about the role of the guitar with a pianist. In an interview that the author conducted in 1996 in Boston, Carlos said that:

> Sometimes it's best not to play during the piano solo because you can't be a mind reader, I don't know when he will start comping out and then what I will play will clash. So, I never play during the piano solo." Later, when asked about comping in a group setting, he states "I like to pull ideas from the ambiance. I never like to do the same thing every day. I like to play more like a *conguero*[8]—it's good to know about all the instruments and rhythms going on in the group. You must know about the music before playing it.[9]

Carlos' sound is characterized by both a clean jazz sound and wah wah and distortion guitar "a la Santana." Check out Carlos on the Latin jazz version of "Stella by Starlight," aka "Estella va Estallar"[10].

Bobby Redfield

According to an interview conducted by Antonie Boessenkool for the Orange County Register with S. Duncan Reid, who interviewed Redfield extensively for his book *Cal Tjader: The Life and Recordings of the Man Who Revolutionized Latin Jazz*.[11]

> Reid states that guitar is not a typical instrument for Latin jazz playing. But with Tjader's inclusion of Redfield in his band, guitar was incorporated into the Latin jazz sound. "He (Bobby) was the only regular guitar player in any of Cal's Latin jazz bands. He was very proud of that," Reid said. "He really brought the guitar into that sound, and it wasn't really something you would

---

8 Conguero means conga player.

9 Morales, Carlos Emilio, interview by Neff Irizarry II. *Afro Cuban Guitar* Berklee College of Music Bachelors Degree Thesis (May 20, 1996).

10 Irakere, "Irakere - Estela Va Estallar," posted by Raul Rico, Nov 13, 2014, YouTube video, 10:01, https://www.youtube.com/watch?v=y8ztP6awsIY.

11 S. Duncan Reid, *Cal Tjader: The Life and Recordings of the Man Who Revolutionized Latin Jazz*, (McFarland and company, Incorporated publishers 2013).

hear in most Latin jazz bands. He was unique, different. He innovated in a lot of ways.[12]

Bobby Redfield innovated the way that guitar interacted between the vibraphone and piano in a Latin jazz format. His guitar playing reflects his tasteful listening abilities to leave space for the piano while still playing the traditional *guajeos* with the pianist. Clare Fischer's son, Brent Fischer, further substantiates this in the following excerpt from our interview.

> Well, Cal had a guitarist, Bobby Redfield. Bobby was one of those tasty players who just understood what my dad did and he kind of stayed out of the way when he needed to. I'm not sure if that's where it evolved from, but eventually my father developed the idea of the guitar as functioning, at least in his groups, as an ensemble instrument rather than a rhythm instrument. I think this is the most important point: once he started considering it an ensemble instrument, it was something where he wanted to write parts for the guitar to play, just as he was considering a part for the sax or any of the other horns. They each had a specific function and none of them necessarily played through the whole song either. Horns play their parts, have changes for solos and get a chance to rest. So the way it developed for him was that he noticed Bobby Redfield would just lay out sometimes and let my dad take over comping, especially when he saw him doing something really unusual. On the other hand, there were times when Dad would lay out and he would hand it off to Bobby and then Bobby would take over and do his thing. And so it developed into a situation where he felt that, in this way, whoever was comping the chords could be really free to throw in whatever types of voicings that they wanted, however unusual or intricate. Because there wasn't a second person comping chords at the same time, you didn't have to worry about coordination of voicings and ideas, things like that, especially with chromatic alterations.[13]

---

[12] Antonie Boessenkool, "Bobby Redfield, Guitarist from O.C.," The Orange County Register, July 8, 2015, https://www.ocregister.com/2015/01/08/bobby-redfield-latin-jazz-guitarist-from-oc/.

[13] Brent Fischer, interview by Neff Irizarry II. *Brent Fischer on Clare Fischer's unique concept for the guitar* (April 28th, 2020).

Bobby's contributions can be heard on "Puttin it Together," "Guarabe," and "Cuban Fantasy."

Carlos Santana

Carlos' influence in establishing Latin guitar to the forefront of popular mainstream culture makes him a crucial part of the discussion of the role of electric guitar in Afro-Cuban and Latin jazz music. Although one might not associate Carlos as a jazz guitarist because of his sound and improvisational vocabulary, he did help to establish the guitar's voice in Latin music and Latin jazz with his popular appeal. It is also important to note the achievements of his late brother Jorge Santana with the Fania All Stars.

Carlos took the repertoire of Latin jazz such as "Oye Como Va," "Maria Caracoles," "Bacalao con Pan" and "Evil Ways" and mixed it with the distorted rock sound, which helped the guitar yet again come to the foreground. His concept of mixing blues/rock guitar with Afro-Cuban rhythms influenced his contemporaries such as Jorge Santana, Elliot Randall, Jerry Garcia, Carlos Emilio "El Gordo" Morales, Bobby Redfield, Edgardo Miranda, Jorge Chicoy and Steve Khan. The overdriven, distorted sound became yet another tool for the Latin jazz guitarist to utilize and emulate.

Steve Khan

Considered as "The voice of Latin jazz on guitar" in the modern era according to *Músico Pro* magazine, the modern-day contribution of Steve Khan to the development of the role of the electric guitar in Latin jazz is unparalleled. His unique chordal and melodic approach and profound understanding of Latin music allow Steve to shed new light upon something that is otherwise scarce in Latin jazz. A brief analysis of his approach is on pages 159-161.

From private conversations with Steve spanning over two decades, the author witnessed first-hand the development of the role of the electric guitar in Latin jazz. This influence is prevalent in the artistic and compositional style of the author on display in the concluding sections of this book. Steve states that:

> Guitar does not have a role! A traditional jazz guitar sound cannot sonically cut through Latin percussion in a live environment. There are exceptions to

this, of course, but in the recording studio, anything is possible. For live situations, Santana's sound is, in some ways, the perfect answer.[14]

Steve Khan's development of the role of Latin jazz guitar from *Tightrope* to *Patchwork*[15] is an encyclopedia of how a guitar can function in a trio format with percussion, and this requires an investigation dedicated to his unique harmonic approach to playing *guajeos* and *montunos* on the guitar. Most importantly, Steve was a member of the Caribbean Jazz Project and is featured on two records, *New Horizons*, *Paraiso*, and a live concert, *The Caribbean Jazz Project-Subway 2000*.[16]

---

14 Private conversations with Steve Khan, 1999. Please visit https//:www.stevekhan.com

15 Please see Timeline of Selected Recordings for more information.

16 The Caribbean Jazz Project, "The Caribbean Jazz Project – Subway 2000," posted by uvisniblue, February 10, 2018, YouTube video, 57:48, https://www.youtube.com/watch?v=JqUWu3EImuE.

CHAPTER 6

Latin Jazz and the Jazz Guitarist

In 1940, Dizzy Gillespie and Chano Pozo pioneered Cu-Bop with songs such as "Tin Tin Deo," "Manteca," and "A Night in Tunisia," among others. The fascination and love for Latin music continued throughout the '50s until the present day. "The term Latin jazz was coined during the 1950s by the American media, but it's always been an overly simplistic description of a complex musical melting pot. In truth, that pot has always been a cultural cauldron, and Latin-jazz bandleaders—of both big and small groups—carry on the tradition today by adding ingredients from numerous ancestral countries, as well as drawing influences from the internet and the growing Latino population in the United States."[1]

"As a fledgling term, Latin jazz was lumped into blends of jazz with its two most influential mixers, Afro-Cuban and Brazilian music. Cuban bandleader and arranger Mario Bauzá (who'd already worked with Fletcher Henderson, Cab Calloway and Chick Webb) essentially created Latin jazz in the early 1940s in New York City, fusing jazz arrangements with percussive Afro-Cuban rhythms as musical director for vocalist Machito and his Afro-Cubans big band."[2] However, it is important to note that Latin jazz always had some type of guitarist incorporated in the group, with or without a pianist.

Because of the heightened popularity of Latin music, especially during the aptly-named "Mambo Craze," Tito Puente was able to incorporate the electric guitar with his Big Band recordings because of the backing of RCA. One of the most important records from this period is, perhaps, *Night Beat*, featuring John Quara on "Son de la Loma." How-

---

1 Bill Meredith, "Latin Jazz: The Latin Tinge." *Jazz Times*, November 1, 2007, 20.

2 Bill Meredith, "Latin Jazz: The Latin Tinge." *Jazz Times*, November 1, 2007, 20.

ever, John doesn't solo here and only plays the melody. Bobby Sanabria supports this statement by stating:

> How did Tito Puente get these great studio musicians? They were on staff for RCA but they didn't do the gigs with him. Cuban music was the biggest thing. The only thing that killed it was Elvis Presley in 1956. Then on January 1st 1959, Castro takes over Cuba and they dropped everybody including Puente resulting in Tito going back to Tico records. Bobby asked Puente: why did you use guitars? Tito responded "*pa' jode*r" to try something different. Bobby went on to state that "These guys wanted hit records. They wanted things that resonated with the public.[3]

The electric guitar was extremely popular at the time. And, because of its convenience for mobility and intonation, some daring bandleaders chose to use the guitar rather than have the inconvenience of tuning an acoustic piano before every gig.

Not all of the guitarists were Latinos, nor did they have a deep understanding of Latin music. Their understanding of key Latin rhythms is debatable amongst some experts. However, from my observations, they used their supreme talent and musical sense to cope with the *clave, cáscara, tumbao* and *guajeo/montuno* as naturally as possible.

These classic bebop guitarists from 1950-1970 include Barney Kessel, Jimmy Raney, Grant Green, Wes Montgomery, Kenny Burrell, Attila Zoller, Eddie Duran, George Benson, John Quara, Barry Galbraith, and Everette Barksdale. Their means of playing Latin jazz included Afro-Cuban versions of jazz standards or selections from the well-known Latin repertoire of the time. From my observations of the pieces during this time, there are six common characteristics in arrangement and improvisation that the guitarist used:

- Latin head, jazz swing solo section
- Latin head and Latin solo
- Specific parts arranged for the guitarist
- Soloing with regard to one of the Afro-Cuban rhythms present

---

[3] Bobby Sanabria, interview by Neff Irizarry II. *The Role of the Guitar in Latin Jazz* (April 3, 2020).

CHAPTER 6 — LATIN JAZZ AND THE JAZZ GUITARIST

- Swing eighth-note rhythmic approach
- Soloing without regard to the Afro-Cuban rhythms present

Barney Kessel: *Contemporary Latin Rhythms* highlights Barney Kessel playing five songs in an Afro-Cuban setting. Barney solos over an Afro-Cuban rhythmic feel in all songs.

- "The Peanut Vendor" (El Manicero) - Mambo with a bossa nova ostinato pattern
- "Quizás Quizás Quizás" - Mambo with a bossa nova ostinato pattern
- "Love" - Afro 6/8 and fast samba
- "Latin Dance no.1" 2:3 - Mambo
- "Blues in the Night" - 6/8 bembe and swing

Grant Green: *The Latin Bit* highlights Grant Green playing four songs in an Afro-Cuban setting. However, his solos are over a straight ahead jazz feel.

- "Bésame Mucho" (Bolero)
- "Mambo Inn" (Mambo)
- "My Little Suede Shoes" (Mambo)
- "Hey There" (Bolero)

Wes Montgomery

- "Cariba" from *Full House Recorded Live at Tsubo*

CHAPTER 6 — LATIN JAZZ AND THE JAZZ GUITARIST

©1965 Renewed Taggie Music Co., a division of Gopam Enterprises, Inc. Used by Permission

"Cariba" characterizes the propensity of the time period in Latin jazz, where elements of Afro-Cuban and Brazilian styles were mixed together. Notice the melodic rhythm's similarities with the *clave* and *cáscara* patterns. In my opinion, this era of Latin jazz becomes rhythmically quite unclear and sometimes speculatory due to the experimentation and hybrid fusion of styles occurring so rampantly.

CHAPTER 6

LATIN JAZZ AND THE JAZZ GUITARIST

Kenny Burrell

CONTEMPORARY LATIN JAZZ GUITAR, VOL. 1

CHAPTER 6
LATIN JAZZ AND THE JAZZ GUITARIST

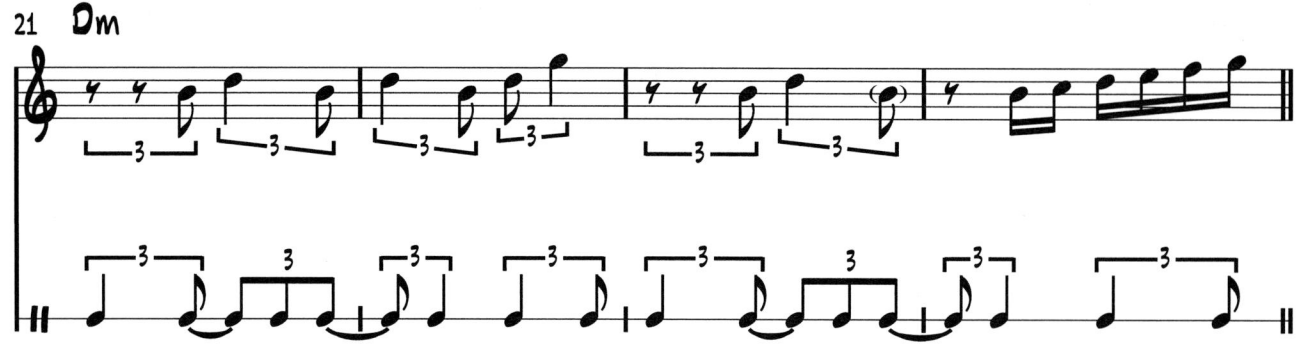

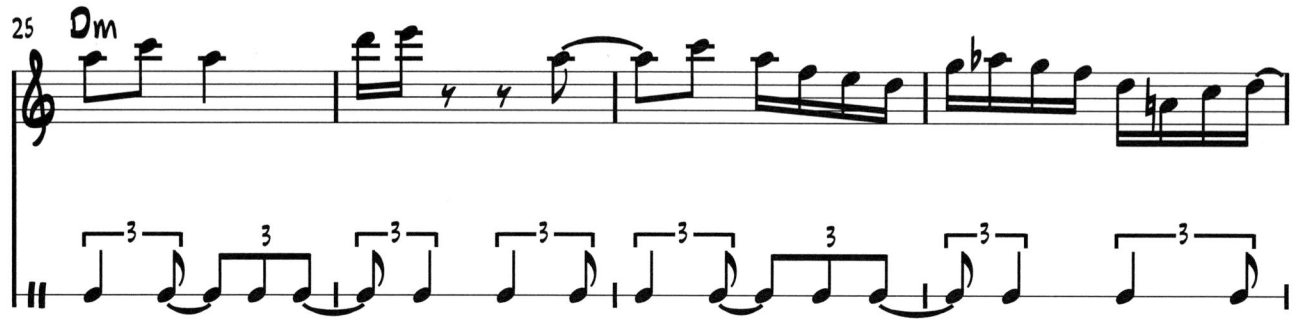

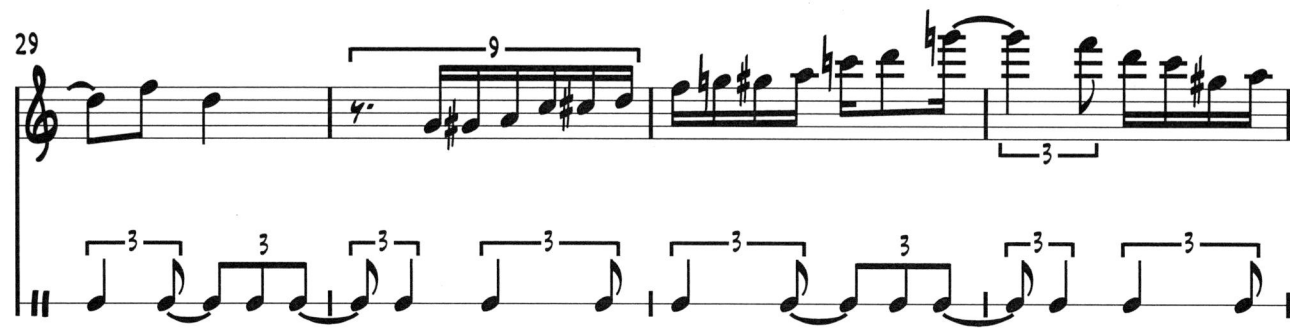

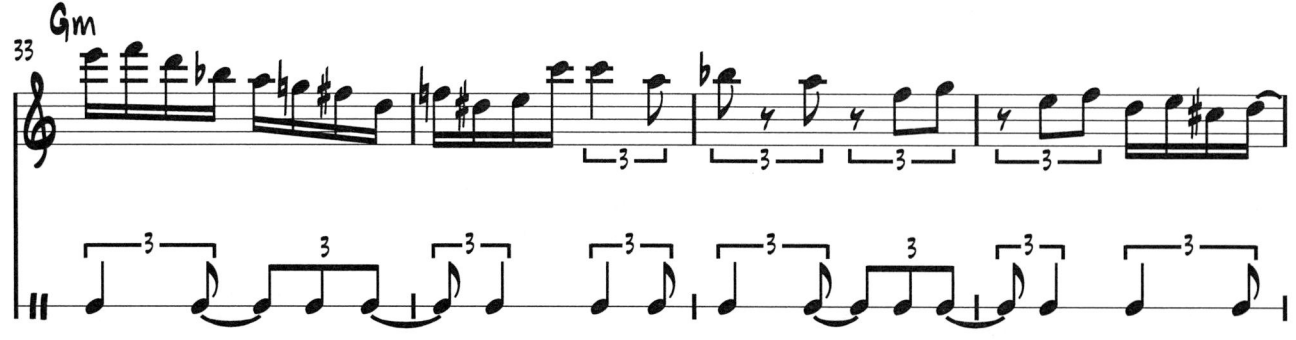

CHAPTER 6

LATIN JAZZ AND THE JAZZ GUITARIST

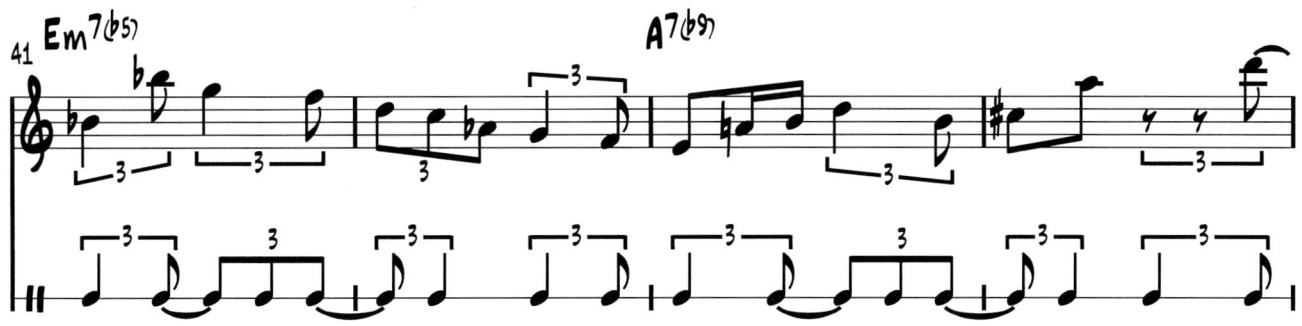

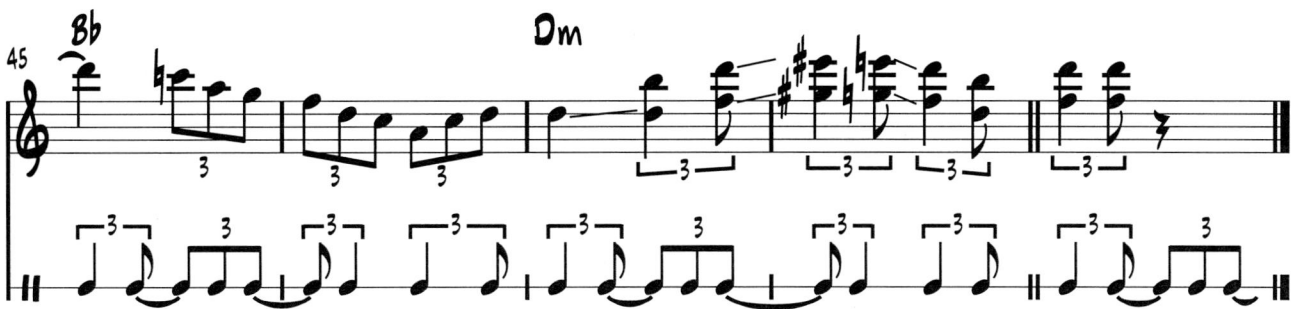

Besides the impeccable, bluesy note choice and chromatic lines consistent with jazz guitar, one must pay close attention to how Kenny creates rhythmic tension against the 6/8 clave. Although Kenny doesn't play any *guajeos or montunos*, he does manage to solidify his 4/4 swing rhythmic feel while accenting the 6/8 clave.

Attila Zoller

If you listen closely to Attila's solo you will notice how he is phrasing consistently with the 8th note conga *marcha* pattern in the mambo style. Please note that these are the standard solo changes for "Manteca" and do not reflect the embellished harmonizations that Chick Corea plays during Attila's solo.

CHAPTER 6

LATIN JAZZ AND THE JAZZ GUITARIST

"Manteca"
Attila Zoller Solo 02:30–03:06
Cal Tjader *Soul Burst*

BAUZÁ

CHAPTER 6
LATIN JAZZ AND THE JAZZ GUITARIST

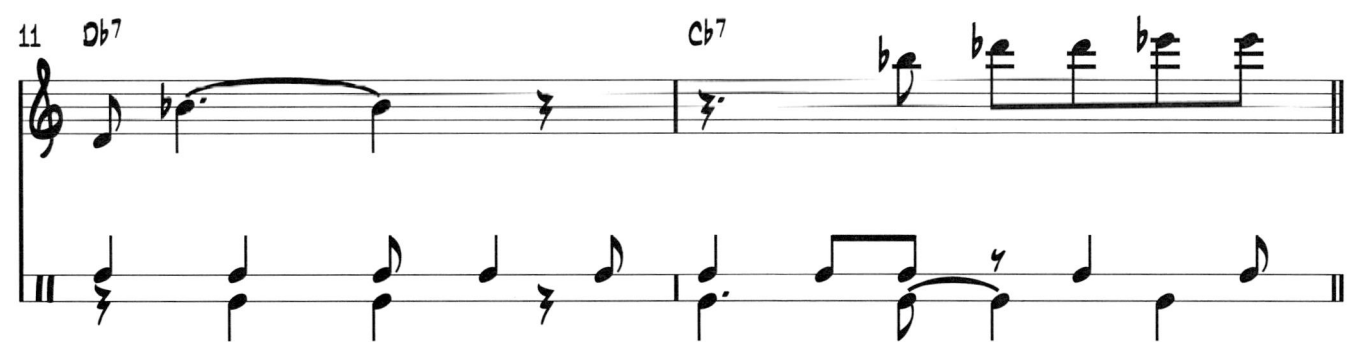

CONTEMPORARY LATIN JAZZ GUITAR, VOL. 1

CHAPTER 6

LATIN JAZZ AND THE JAZZ GUITARIST

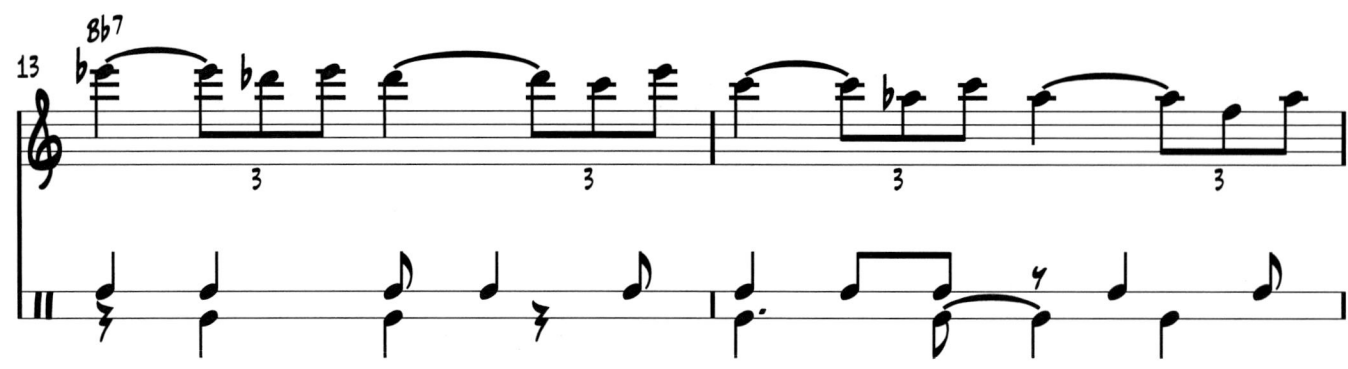

146

CONTEMPORARY LATIN JAZZ GUITAR, VOL. 1

CHAPTER 6 　　　　　　　　　　　　　　　　　LATIN JAZZ AND THE JAZZ GUITARIST

Also, notice how he occasionally accents the 2 side of the *clave* and sometimes even anticipates the *tumbao* and *cáscara* patterns.

CHAPTER 6

LATIN JAZZ AND THE JAZZ GUITARIST

Danny Embrey

148

CONTEMPORARY LATIN JAZZ GUITAR, VOL. 1

CHAPTER 6

LATIN JAZZ AND THE JAZZ GUITARIST

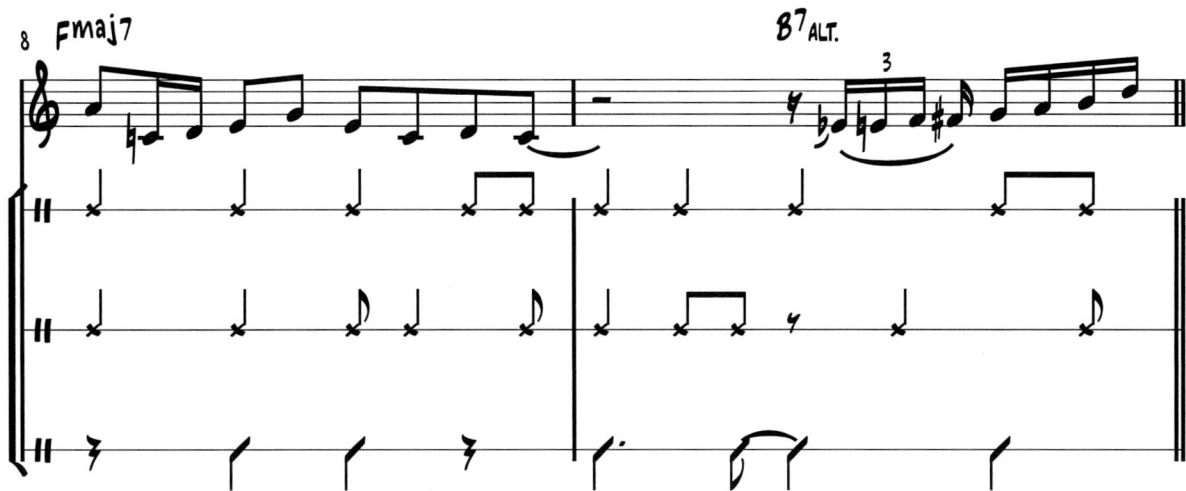

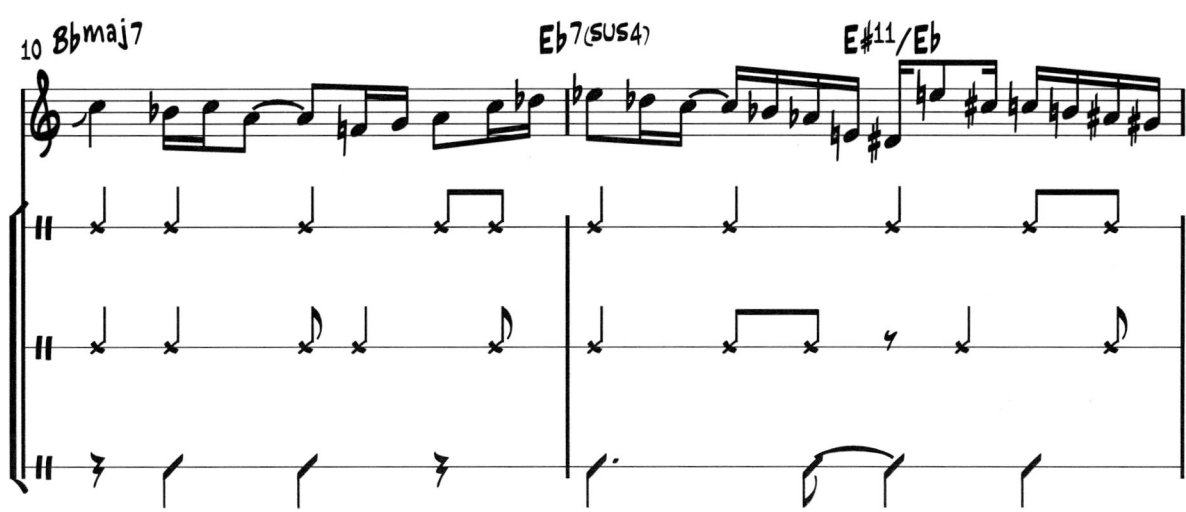

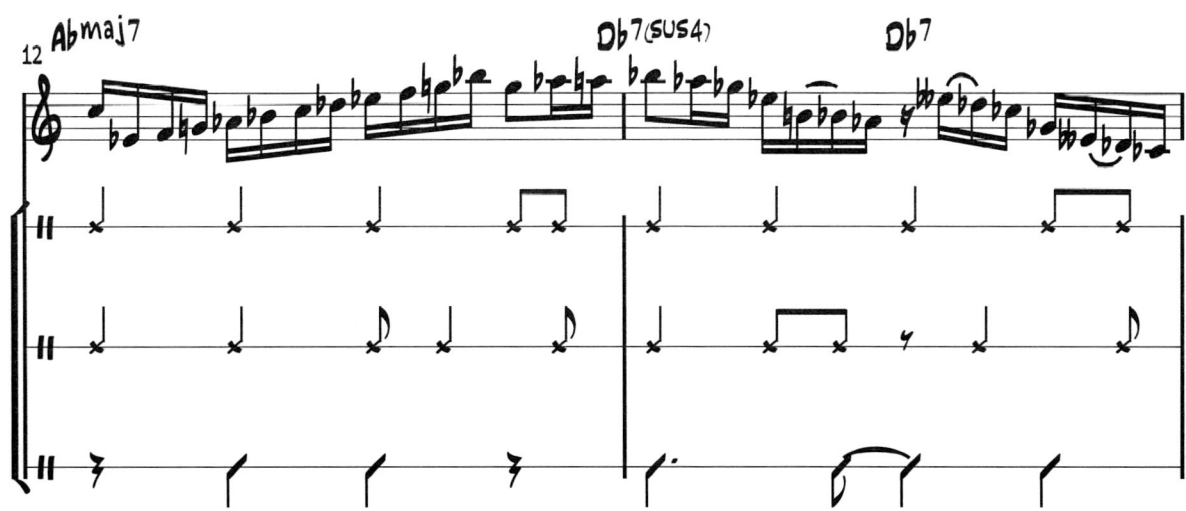

CONTEMPORARY LATIN JAZZ GUITAR, VOL. 1

CHAPTER 6 — LATIN JAZZ AND THE JAZZ GUITARIST

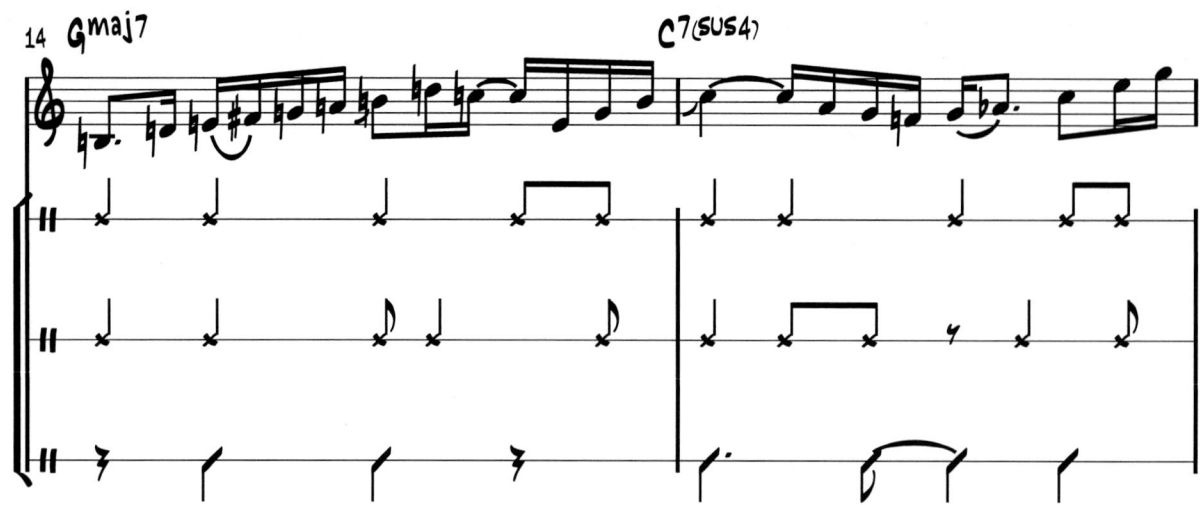

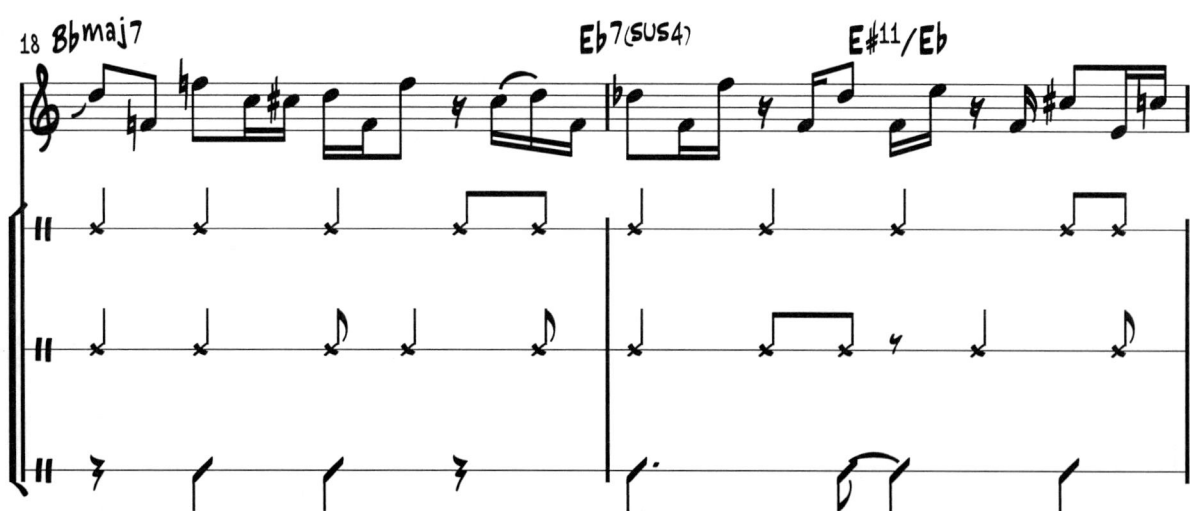

CHAPTER 6

LATIN JAZZ AND THE JAZZ GUITARIST

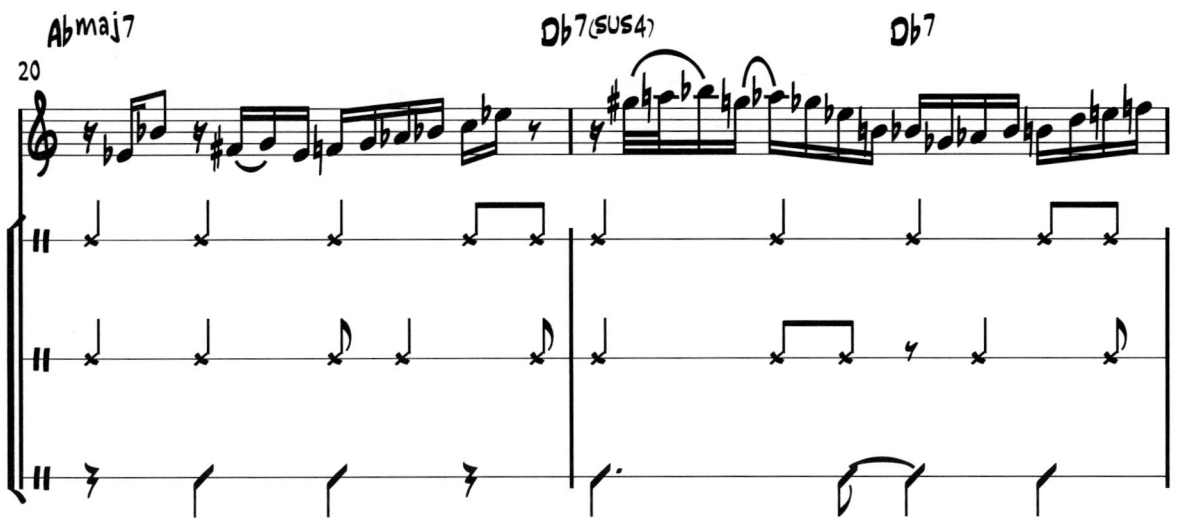

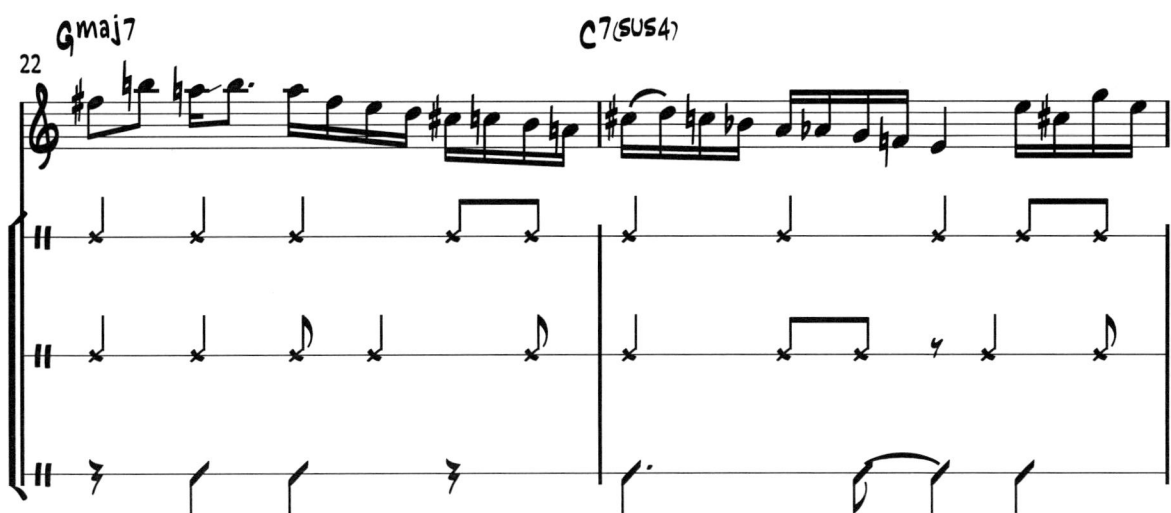

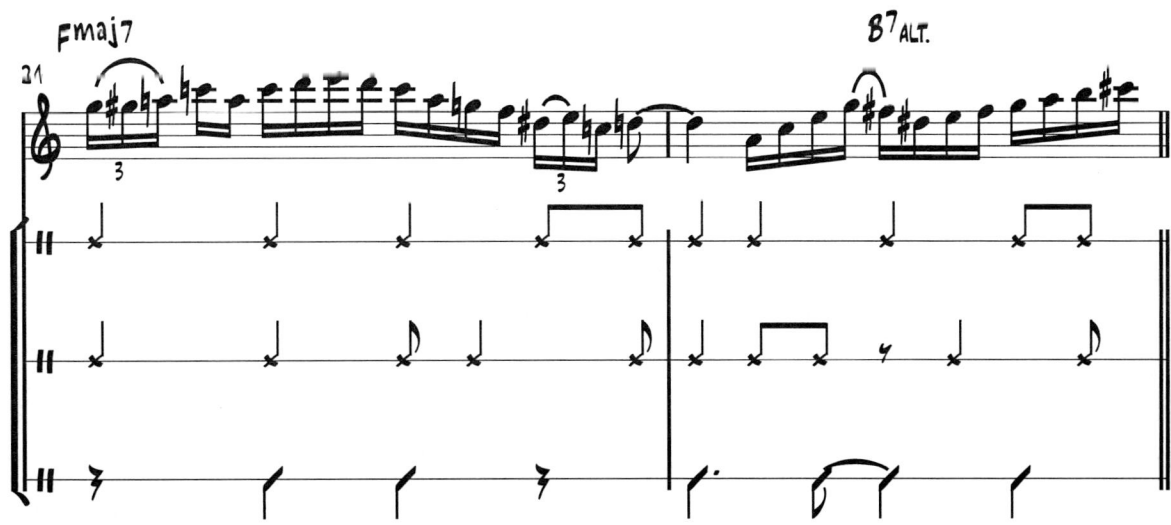

CONTEMPORARY LATIN JAZZ GUITAR, VOL. 1

CHAPTER 6

LATIN JAZZ AND THE JAZZ GUITARIST

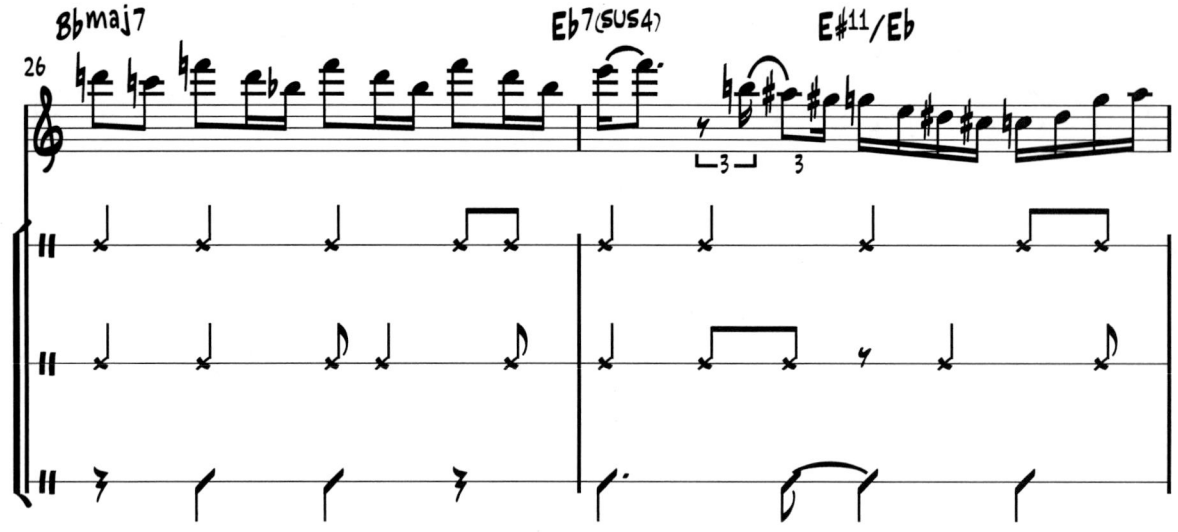

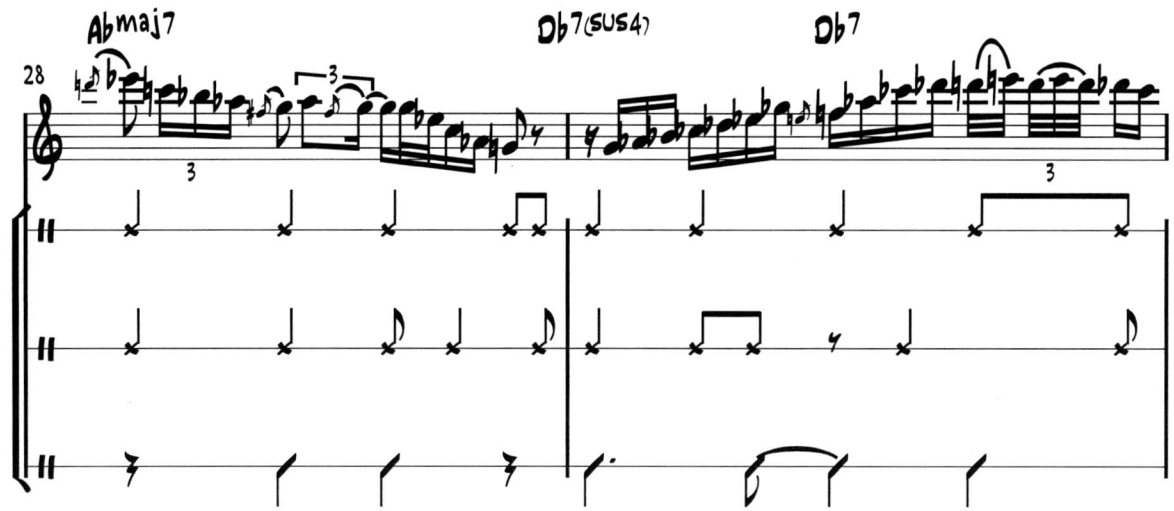

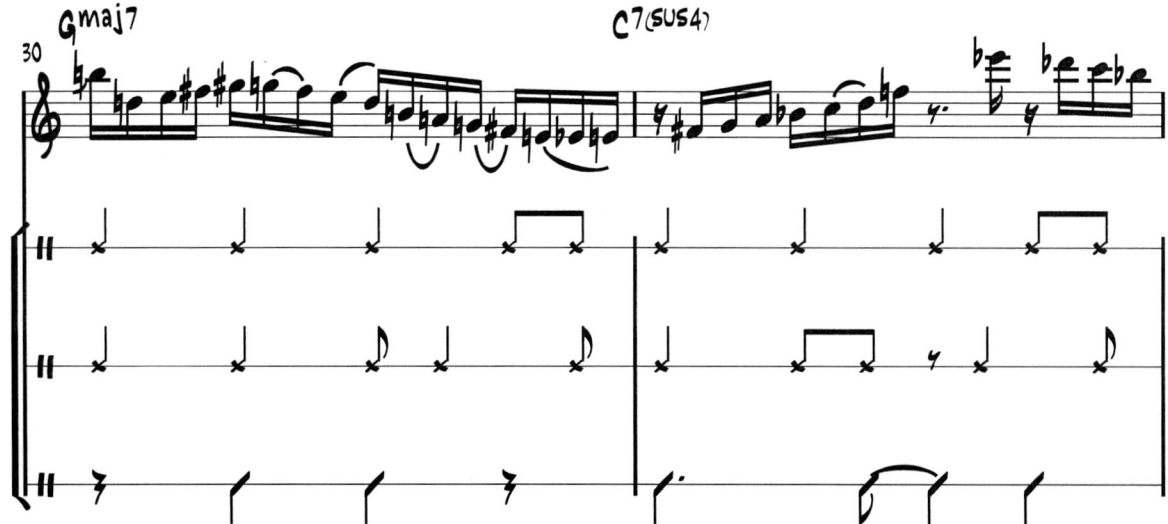

152   CONTEMPORARY LATIN JAZZ GUITAR, VOL. 1

CHAPTER 6 — LATIN JAZZ AND THE JAZZ GUITARIST

Danny plays typical Wes Montgomery and Pat Martino-inspired lines that are consistent with the bell pattern for cha-cha-chá, while also anticipating his phrases in measure 10-15 using the rhythm of Clare Fischer's *montuno* pattern. Measure 18 provides a unique instance where Danny plays a figure that adds *tres*-style *guajeo,* angular and polyrhythmic tension against the *montuno* pattern. Because of the constant sixteenth-note rhythmic choice that doesn't align with any fixed pattern of the style, Danny adds articulation through octave displacement, accents, and syncopation, so that his phrasing is aligned with some parts of the key patterns.

Although what these jazz guitarists played might not be completely stylistically consistent, the solos do show that articulation and rhythmic choice are a defining element in the success of their improvisations.

From my observations, I have found that the jazz guitarists featured here did in fact react under the influence of the style in the following ways by articulating these key rhythms:

- Conga or bell pattern
- *Cáscara*
- *Clave*
- *Tumbao*

CHAPTER 6 — LATIN JAZZ AND THE JAZZ GUITARIST

When it wasn't possible to articulate these key patterns, then jazz guitarists:

- Change the solo section to swing (in some cases)
- Specific parts were written for them

The focus of these featured solos is on the rhythmic choices the bebop guitarists made. In some cases, they didn't accent the *clave, cáscara* or *tumbao* in order to favor the bebop harmonic and rhythmic language. However, this bebop improvisational language, with the use of sophisticated harmonic chord substitutions and chromaticism, set the standard for all guitar players to come. The melodic and harmonic content will be covered in the next volume.

CHAPTER 7
Improvisation, Transcription and Analysis

In a soloist capacity, the guitar in Latin jazz can either function as another horn doubling melodic parts, or by using improvisation. Previous examples displayed Sonny Henry doing so, and Paul Alicea displayed the same traits on "La Playa Fantasy." However, what is the definition of stylistic consistency in Latin jazz?

An improviser must play effortlessly with accentuation of the *clave, cáscara* and *tumbao* patterns and Afro-Cuban rhythms in general. This doesn't mean, however, that they have to only play those patterns. In order for it to be Latin jazz, the improviser incorporates harmonic and melodic devices from jazz, such as chromaticism and standard harmony relevant to jazz, such as II-V-I or I-VI-II-V progressions. The following examples display these traits in detail.

CHAPTER 7 — IMPROVISATION, TRANSCRIPTION AND ANALYSIS

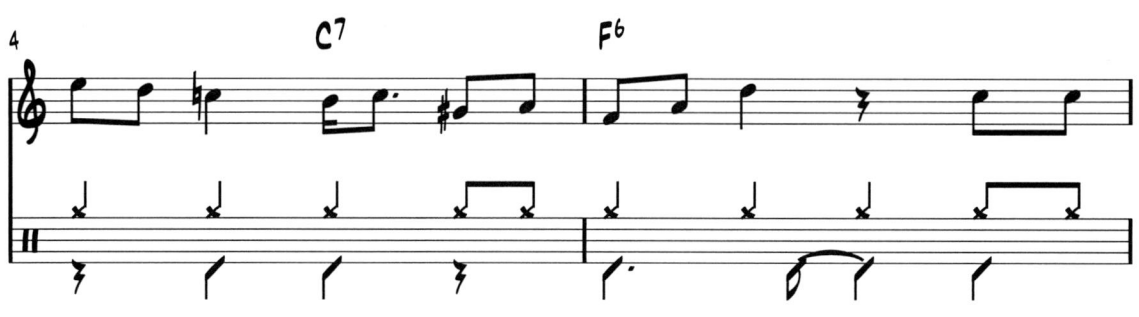

CHAPTER 7 — IMPROVISATION, TRANSCRIPTION AND ANALYSIS

Paul Alicea displays diatonic and chromatic clarity and rhythmic consistency with the emphasis on the two eighth-note pickups on beat four that define the bass pattern in cha-cha-chá. His use of bebop-like scales in bars 3, 4, and 8 shows the jazz influence, while the rhythmic emphasis shadows the cowbell pattern.

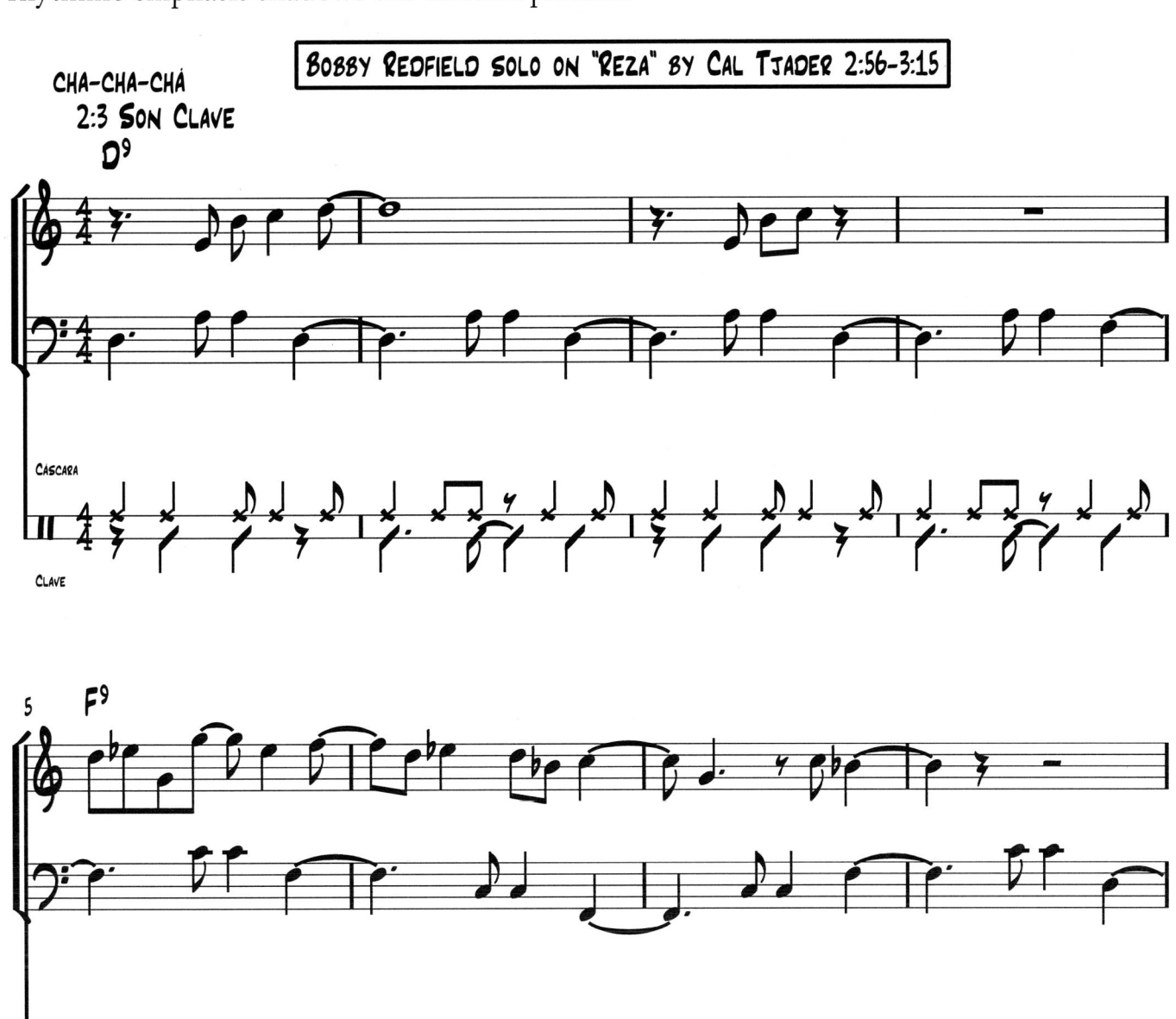

Bobby Redfield displays rhythmic consistency with emphasis on the *cáscara* and *tumbao* patterns. Redfield opens his solo with a rhythmic and melodic fragment constructed upon the *guajeo* pattern over a two-bar phrase. He then contrasts that with an intervallic, angular four-bar phrase with wide intervals in bar 5, and then a contraction of the interval in bars 9-12.

CHAPTER 7 — IMPROVISATION, TRANSCRIPTION AND ANALYSIS

Edgardo Miranda displays rhythmic consistency, polyrhythmic tension, and the use of the tritone substitution of F#7 over the C7 vamp. Edgardo also uses chromatic approaches during the solo, as well as the use of the triad voice lead to a pentatonic figure in bars 11 & 12. This highlights a sophisticated jazz language coupled with a sophisticated rhythmic understanding on display in bar 5 with a quadruplet and triplet figure.

CONTEMPORARY LATIN JAZZ GUITAR, VOL. 1

CHAPTER 7 — IMPROVISATION, TRANSCRIPTION AND ANALYSIS

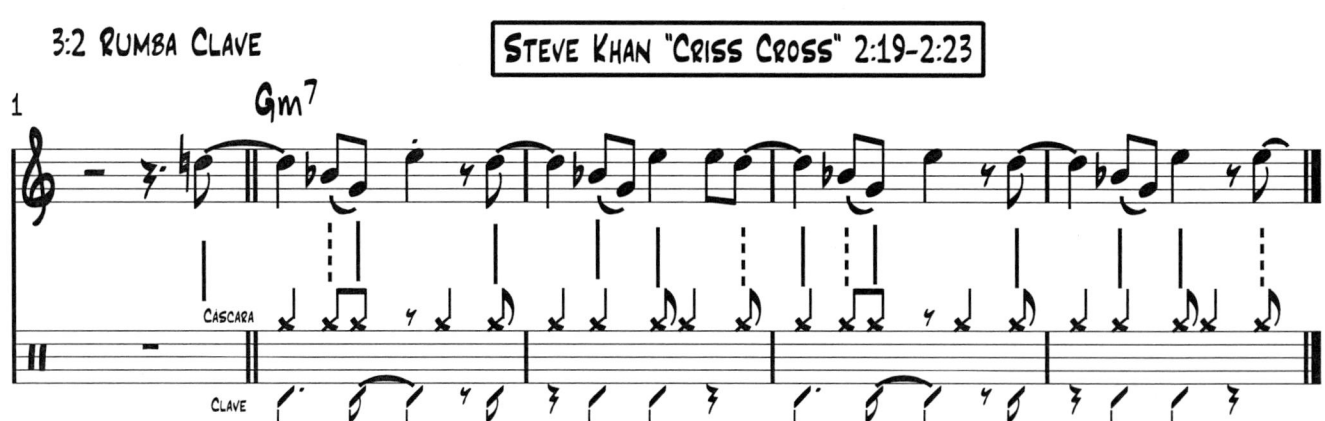

Steve Khan's improvisational technique is even more challenging because of the absence of any harmonic instruments. "Hackensack" demonstrates a clever *guajeo* that alternates between minor seconds, a sixth and a fifth. His use of quartal harmony and

CHAPTER 7 — IMPROVISATION, TRANSCRIPTION AND ANALYSIS

chord voicings in "Criss Cross" exhibit another level of sophistication that is his own. But, he has a rhythmic consistency that adheres to the *clave, cáscara* and *tumbao* too. This solid rhythmic approach is marked in all three examples in order to show how the precise synchronization with the *clave and cáscara* (broken and solid vertical lines) happen.

Notice again how his note choice provides harmonic clarity throughout with the use of chord tones and tensions with logical voice-leading, as exhibited in the last two bars of the middle example of "Criss Cross."

The next transcription, "Gracinha," was recorded and featured in Steve Khan's book *Contemporary Chord Khancepts*. Steve's solo demonstrates his stylistic rhythmic control, which enables him to accent different parts of the *clave, cáscara* and *tumbao* rhythms while not completely limiting himself to just one rhythm. This advanced way of rhythmical phrasing allows freedom of expression. Although most players are not consciously aware of it, the overwhelming coincidence of rhythmical alignment can't just be left to chance or luck. I believe that in some ways, Steve was conscious and felt the *clave, cáscara* and *tumbao*.

For the next exercise/transcription, "Gracinha," I have only written 2:3 *son clave*. I suggest that you take the time to analyze this solo and circle the passages that show alignment with the *clave, cáscara* and *tumbao* patterns. How does Steve accent them? How can you take some of these techniques and use them in your own playing?

CHAPTER 7 IMPROVISATION, TRANSCRIPTION AND ANALYSIS

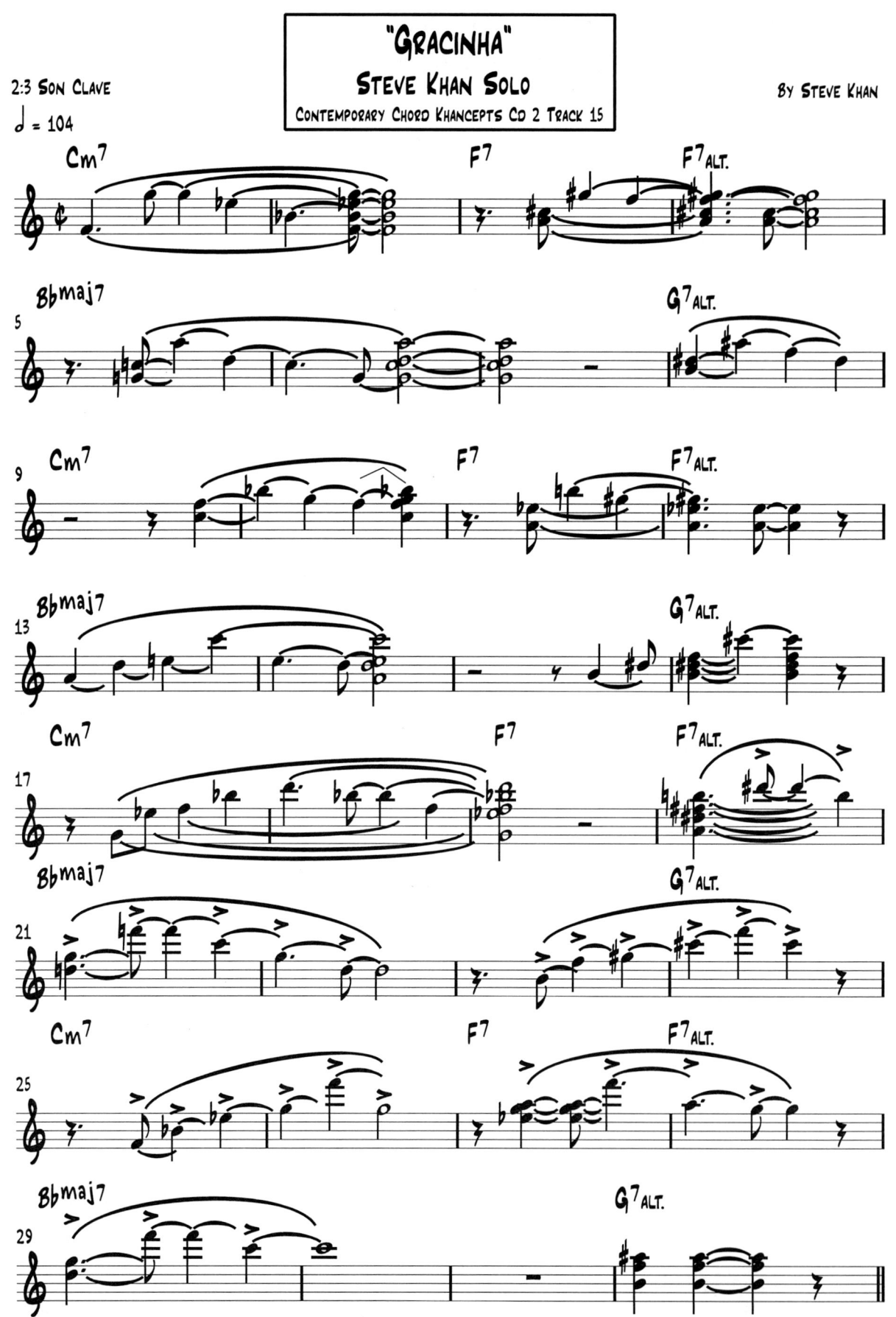

162 CONTEMPORARY LATIN JAZZ GUITAR, VOL. 1

CHAPTER 7
IMPROVISATION, TRANSCRIPTION AND ANALYSIS

CONTEMPORARY LATIN JAZZ GUITAR, VOL. 1

CHAPTER 7
IMPROVISATION, TRANSCRIPTION AND ANALYSIS

CHAPTER 7
IMPROVISATION, TRANSCRIPTION AND ANALYSIS

CONTEMPORARY LATIN JAZZ GUITAR, VOL. 1

CHAPTER 7 — IMPROVISATION, TRANSCRIPTION AND ANALYSIS

CHAPTER 7
IMPROVISATION, TRANSCRIPTION AND ANALYSIS

During fade out.............

CONTEMPORARY LATIN JAZZ GUITAR, VOL. 1

CHAPTER 8
Compositions and Play-Along Tracks

Now that you have studied the basic patterns and looked at how the foundational guitarists executed *guajeos* and *montunos* in the style, let's apply that knowledge to a typical standard progression.

In the examples below, a typical standard jazz chord progression provides the student with an opportunity to hear and feel how the *guajeo* works in a familiar harmonic setting.

Track 337 *Suggested Fingerings found on pages 5–7*

CHAPTER 8 — COMPOSITIONS AND PLAY-ALONG TRACKS

Track 339

Suggested Fingerings found on pages 5–7

Track 341

Suggested Fingerings found on pages 91-92

CHAPTER 8 — COMPOSITIONS AND PLAY-ALONG TRACKS

In Tracks 337-341, the melody is introduced and phrased in *clave* and *cáscara*. In Track 337, the *guajeo* pattern is played as single-notes. In Track 339, a string grouping technique that utilizes the chord of the moment is employed over the same *guajeo* pattern. In Track 341, an imitation of the traditional instrument sound combined with pianistic influences offers an adaptation that fits the guitar.

Once we analyze the examples above for their inherent harmonic content regarding guide-tones and voice-leading, we begin to understand how to apply our own melodic and harmonic choices within Afro-Cuban Latin jazz.

For this purpose, I have included "Virginiarican Blues" once again. As previously mentioned, I make use of a combination of upper structure voicings, standard drop-two voicings, and *guajeo* patterns in the first line guitar part. Notice how I mix three and four-note chordal voicings for four bars and then switch to a pianistic *guajeo/montuno* guitar adaptation for eight bars.

Play the top line as written and then experiment with implementing some of the ideas featured in Tracks 337-341.

CHAPTER 8 COMPOSITIONS AND PLAY-ALONG TRACKS

Track 343

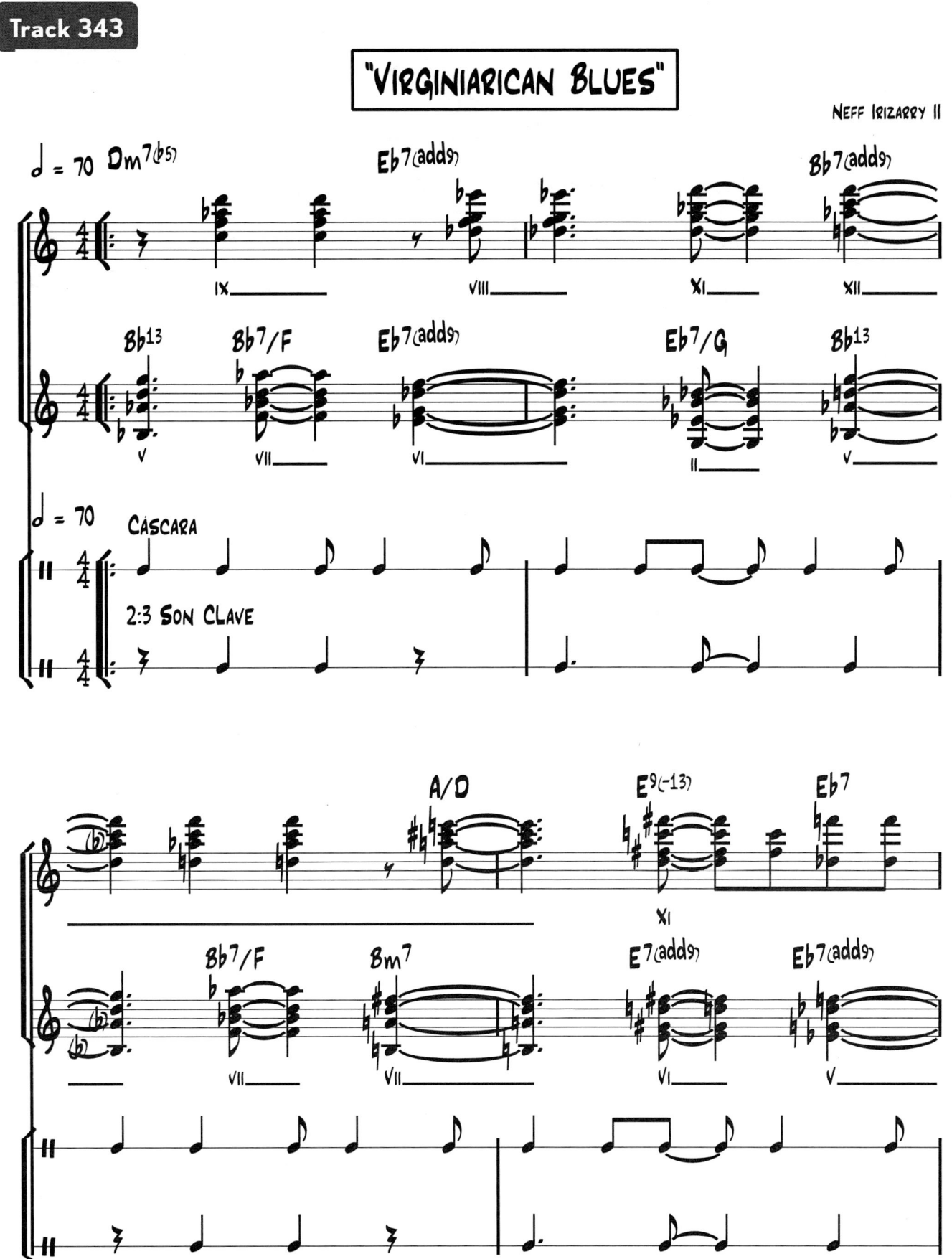

"Virginiarican Blues" — Neff Irizarry II

CONTEMPORARY LATIN JAZZ GUITAR, VOL. 1

171

CHAPTER 8
COMPOSITIONS AND PLAY-ALONG TRACKS

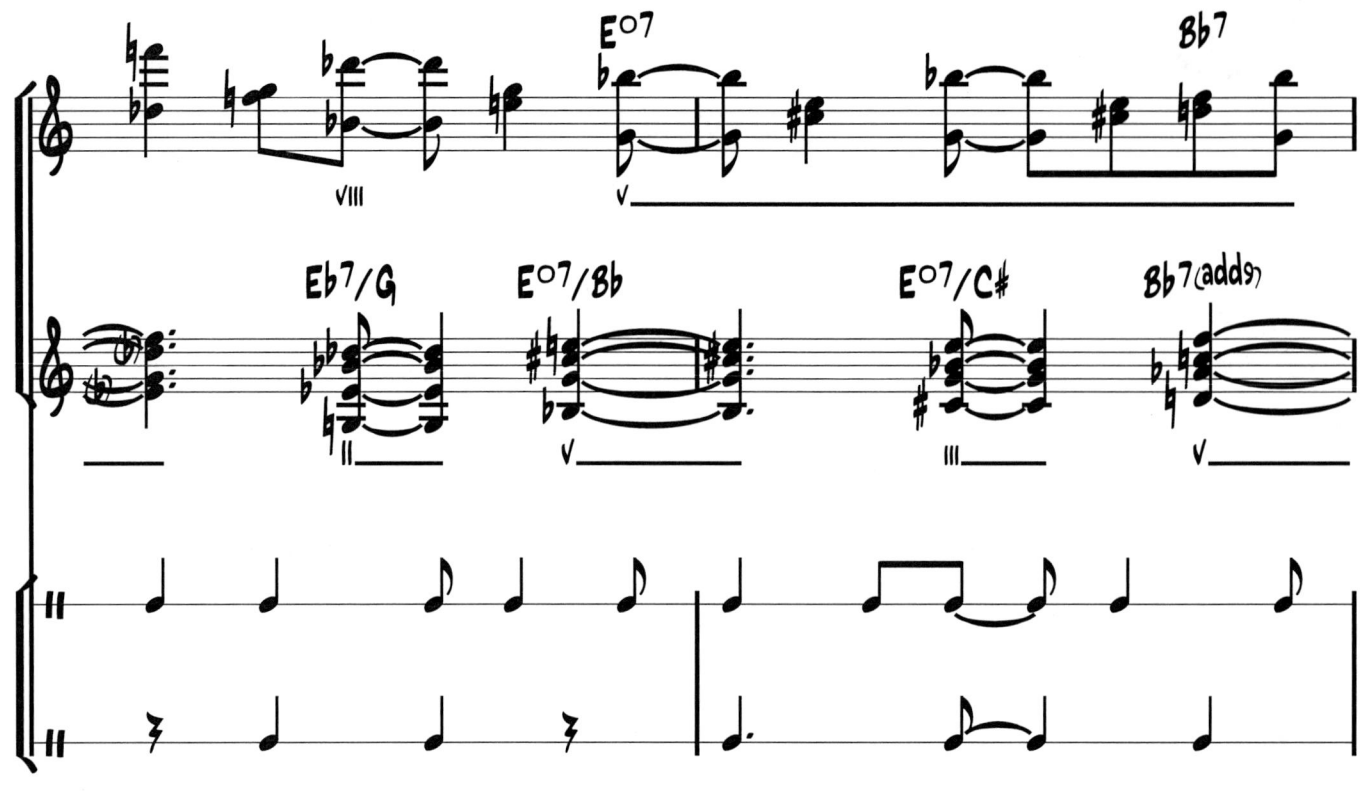

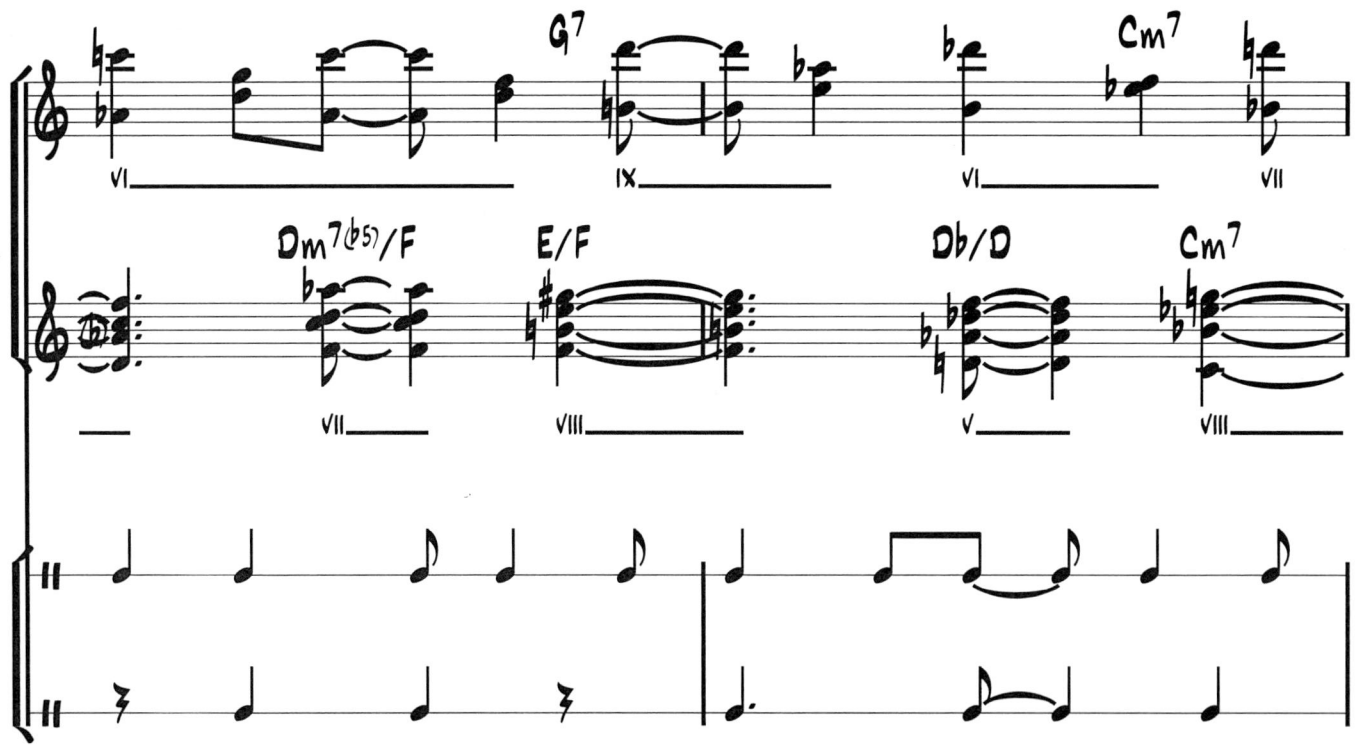

CHAPTER 8
COMPOSITIONS AND PLAY-ALONG TRACKS

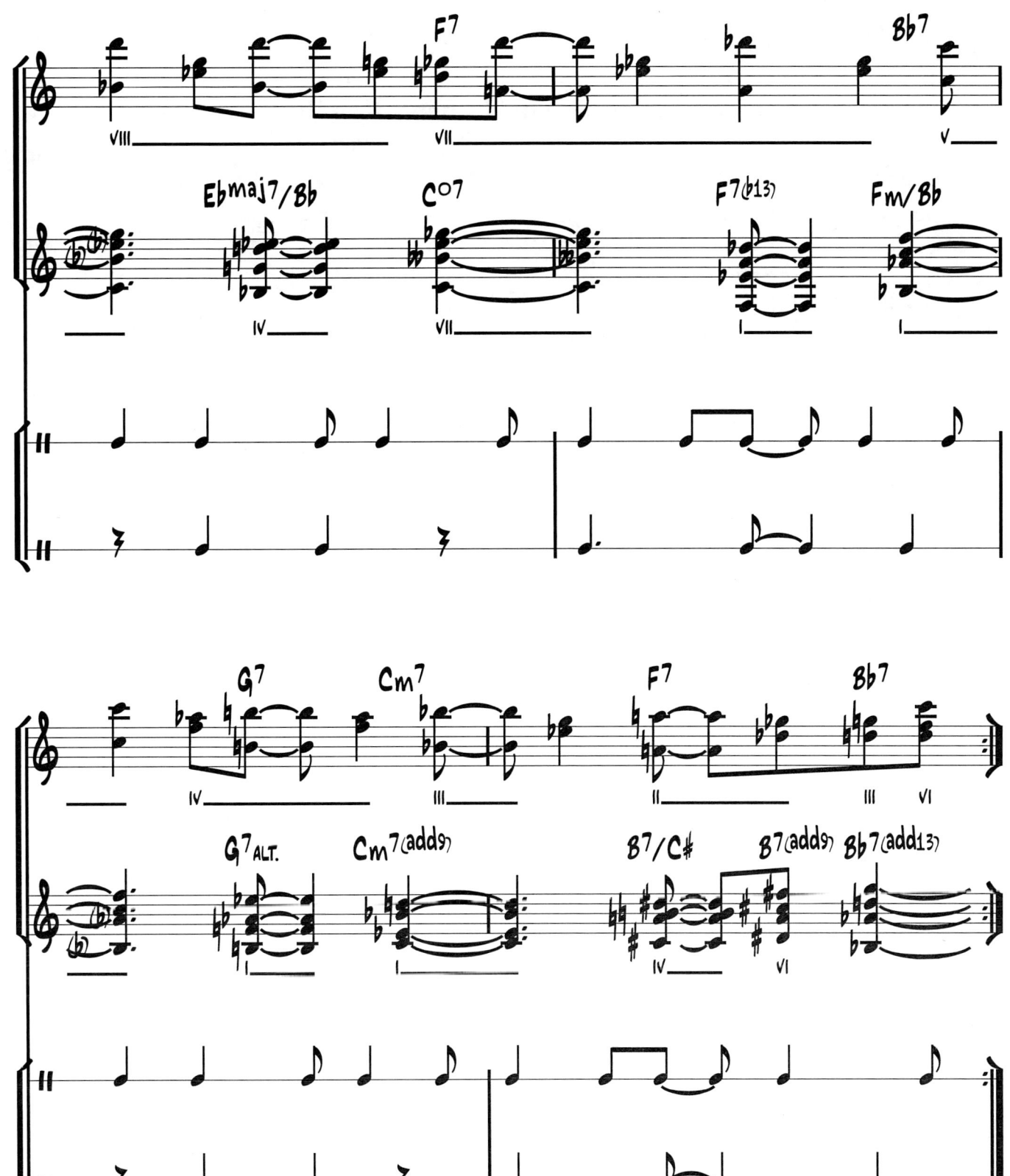

CONTEMPORARY LATIN JAZZ GUITAR, VOL. 1

CHAPTER 8

COMPOSITIONS AND PLAY-ALONG TRACKS

Track 345

Suggested Fingerings found on pages 91-92

Latin Jazz Guitar Arrangement of "Bug in a Rug" by Steve Swallow

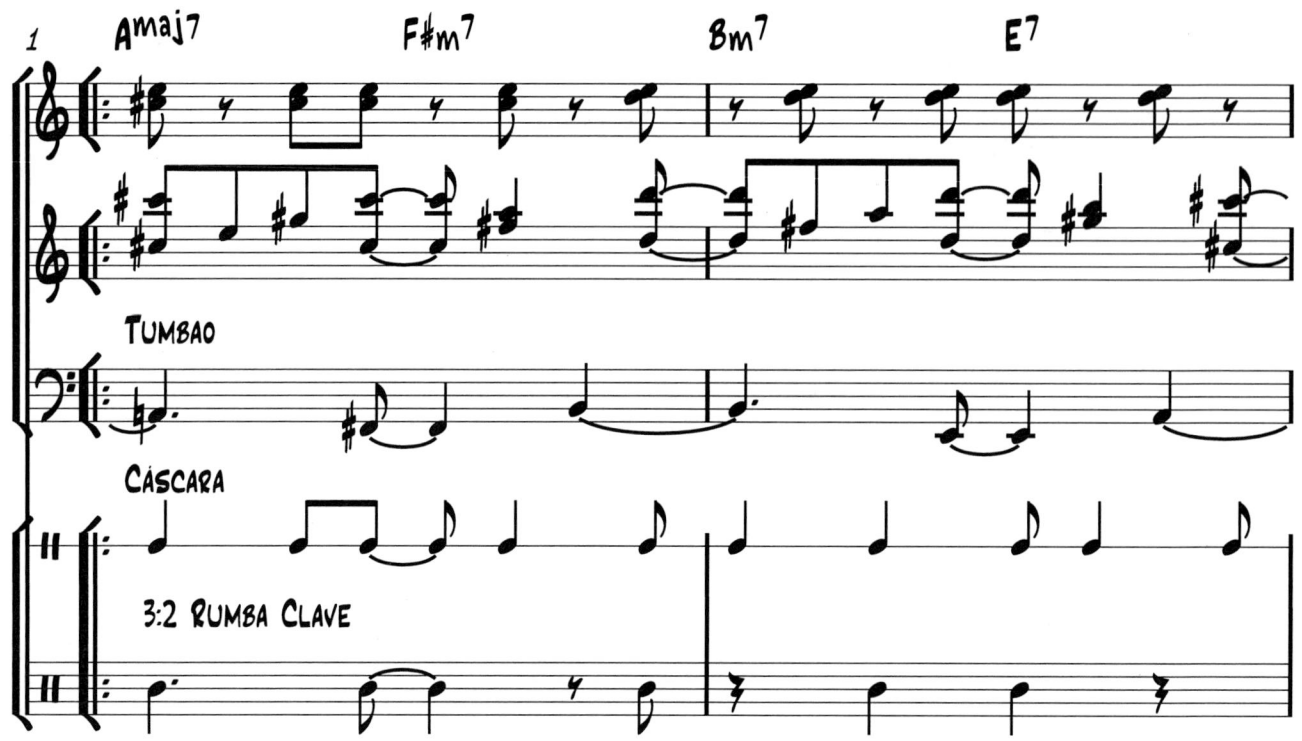

CHAPTER 8

COMPOSITIONS AND PLAY-ALONG TRACKS

©1997 Wonderbuns, Inc. Used by Permission

CHAPTER 8   COMPOSITIONS AND PLAY-ALONG TRACKS

Here's an adaptation of Steve Swallow's composition "Bug in a Rug" that featured Mick Goodrick on guitar. Notice the use of upper structure triads for the *montuno* and that the *montuno* is in *rumba clave* now.

How does this arrangement differ from the original recording? What *guajeo/montuno* techniques are used here? How do these techniques support the melody? How do these techniques rhythmically align with the *clave, cáscara* and *tumbao*?

CHAPTER 8 — COMPOSITIONS AND PLAY-ALONG TRACKS

Play-Along Compositions

Now is the time for you to apply some of these Latin Jazz Guitar concepts over a song. The format for all the songs will be the following:

The first track will be a demonstration and then the second track will be your turn to play the melody, solo, and play *guajeos/montunos* underneath my solo.

Track 347 "El Juego" 2:3 *Rumba Clave*

Tips: Try taking some ideas from the first chorus of "Gracinha" on page 162 or from "Virginiarican Blues" top line guitar part.

Track 349 "Todo lo que fuiste" 2:3 *Rumba Clave*

This track features the changes of a well-known jazz standard.

Tips: Try to play a *guajeo* or *montuno* based on tracks 81–87 (page 23) during the A sections and then tracks 325–331 on the B section found on pages 117–119. Watch out for the tensions on the chords!

Track 351 "Cuando tu no estas" Bolero/Cha-cha-chá

Tips: Try to play the various cha-cha-chá comping ideas found on page 124 and tracks 333–335.

Track 353 "El swing de la finca" Descarga 2:3 *Son Clave*

The intro is in the style of Tito Puente's iconic piece "Rankankan."

Tips: This time, pick your favorite exercises and try to make them work here. Which *guajeo/montuno* technique worked best?

CHAPTER 8

COMPOSITIONS AND PLAY-ALONG TRACKS

Track 347

Form: ABAB Solo section then ABAB to CODA

CHAPTER 8 COMPOSITIONS AND PLAY-ALONG TRACKS

Track 349

Form: AABA. Solos on the form

CHAPTER 8

COMPOSITIONS AND PLAY-ALONG TRACKS

Track 351

Cuando Tú No Estás
When You Are Gone

Bolero/Cha-cha-chá

Neff Irizarry II

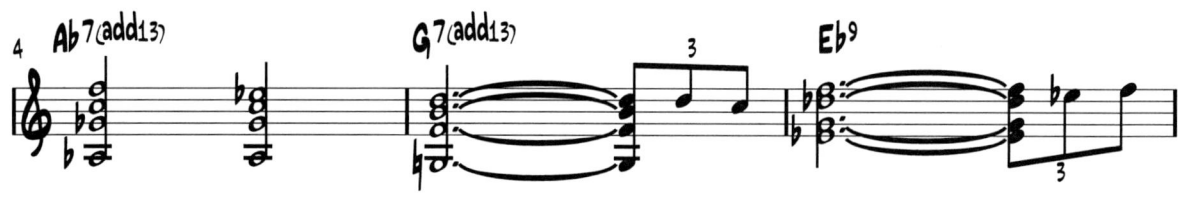

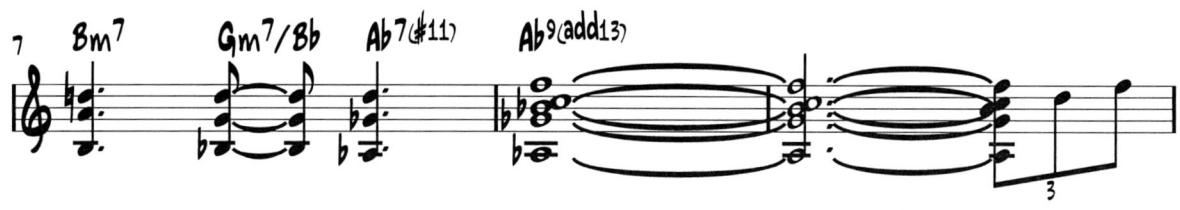

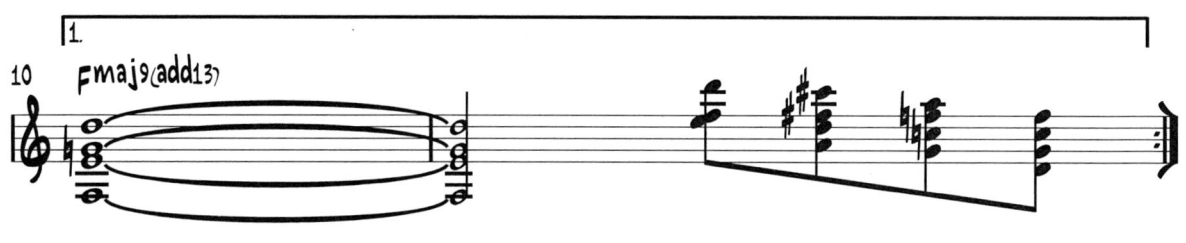

CHAPTER 8
COMPOSITIONS AND PLAY-ALONG TRACKS

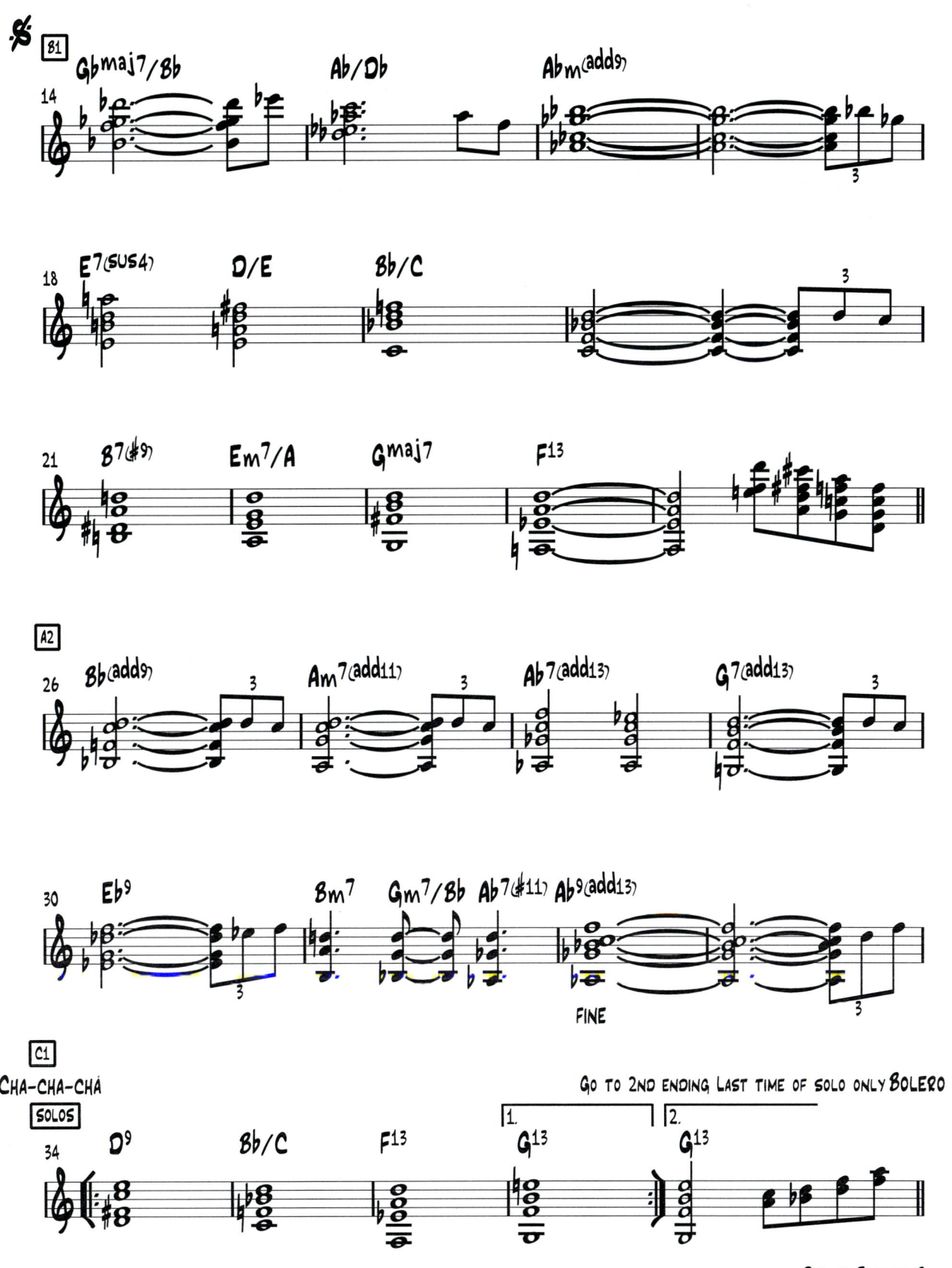

Form: AABA Solo section BA al FINE

CONTEMPORARY LATIN JAZZ GUITAR, VOL. 1

CHAPTER 8

COMPOSITIONS AND PLAY-ALONG TRACKS

Track 353

El Swing de la Finca

DESCARGA
2:3 SON CLAVE

Neff Irizarry II

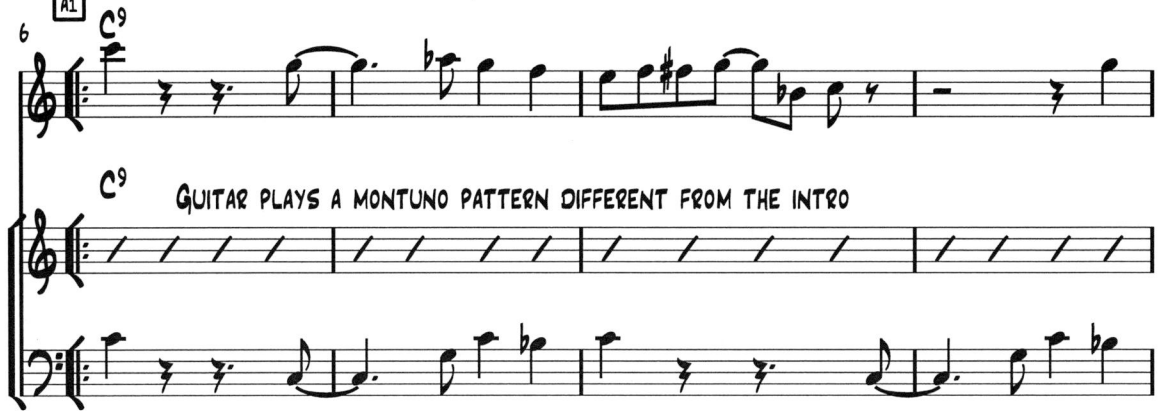

Guitar plays a montuno pattern different from the intro

182   CONTEMPORARY LATIN JAZZ GUITAR, VOL. 1

CHAPTER 8   COMPOSITIONS AND PLAY-ALONG TRACKS

Form: INTRO, A1, B1, A2. Solos: A1, B1, A2, then Intro, A1, B2, A2.

CONTEMPORARY LATIN JAZZ GUITAR, VOL. 1

Play-Along Track List

Track

1	Feeling the subdivision 2:3 *Son Clave*
2	
3	Feeling the subdivision 3:2 *Son Clave*
4	
5	Feeling the subdivision 2:3 *Rumba Clave*
6	
7	Feeling the subdivision 3:2 *Rumba Clave*
8	
9	2:3 *Son Clave* One bar on and off Play the 3 side
10	
11	2:3 *Son Clave* One bar on and off Play the 2 side
12	
13	3:2 *Son Clave* One bar on and off Play the 2 side
14	
15	3:2 *Son Clave* One bar on and off Play the 3 side
16	
17	2:3 *Rumba Clave* One bar on and off Play the 3 side
18	
19	2:3 *Rumba Clave* One bar on and off Play the 2 side
20	
21	3:2 *Rumba Clave* One bar on and off Play the 2 side
22	
23	3:2 *Rumba Clave* One bar on and off Play the 3 side
24	
25	Chords in *Clave* 2:3 *Son Clave* #1
26	
27	Chords in *Clave* 2:3 *Son Clave* #2
28	
29	Chords in *Clave* 2:3 *Son Clave* #3
30	
31	Chords in *Clave* 2:3 *Son Clave* #4
32	
33	Chords in *Clave* 2:3 *Son Clave* #5
34	
35	Chords in *Clave* 2:3 *Son Clave* #6
36	
37	Chords in *Clave* 2:3 *Son Clave* #7
38	
39	Chords in *Clave* 2:3 *Son Clave* #8
40	
41	Chords in *Clave* 3:2 *Son Clave* #9
42	
43	Chords in *Clave* 3:2 *Son Clave* #10
44	
45	Chords in *Clave* 3:2 *Son Clave* #11
46	
47	Chords in *Clave* 3:2 *Son Clave* #12
48	
49	Chords in *Clave* 3:2 *Son Clave* #13
50	
51	Chords in *Clave* 3:2 *Son Clave* #14
52	
53	Chords in *Clave* 3:2 *Son Clave* #15
54	
55	Chords in *Clave* 3:2 *Son Clave* #16
56	
57	Chords in *Clave* 2:3 *Rumba Clave* #17
58	

59	Chords in *Clave* 2:3 *Rumba Clave* #18	93	Implying the *Clave* Advanced 2:3 *Rumba Clave* #35
60			
61	Chords in *Clave* 2:3 *Rumba Clave* #19	94	
62		95	Implying the *Clave* Advanced 3:2 *Rumba Clave* #36
63	Chords in *Clave* 2:3 *Rumba Clave* #20		
64		96	
65	Chords in *Clave* 2:3 *Rumba Clave* #21	97	Feeling the subdivision *Cáscara* 2:3 *Son Clave*
66		98	
67	Chords in *Clave* 2:3 *Rumba Clave* #22	99	Feeling the subdivision *Cáscara* 3:2 *Son Clave*
68			
69	Chords in *Clave* 2:3 *Rumba Clave* #23	100	
70		101	2:3 *Son Clave Cáscara* One bar on and off Play the 3 side #1
71	Chords in *Clave* 2:3 *Rumba Clave* #24		
72		102	
73	Chords in *Clave* 3:2 *Rumba Clave* #25	103	2:3 *Son Clave Cáscara* One bar on and off Play the 2 side #2
74			
75	Chords in *Clave* 3:2 *Rumba Clave* #26	104	
76		105	3:2 *Son Clave Cáscara* One bar on and off Play the 2 side #3
77	Chords in *Clave* 3:2 *Rumba Clave* #27		
78		106	
79	Chords in *Clave* 3:2 *Rumba Clave* #28	107	3:2 *Son Clave Cáscara* One bar on and off Play the 3 side #4
80			
81	Chords in *Clave* 3:2 *Rumba Clave* #29	108	
82		109	Right Hand Independence 2:3 *Son Clave Cáscara* pattern
83	Chords in *Clave* 3:2 *Rumba Clave* #30		
84		110	
85	Chords in *Clave* 3:2 *Rumba Clave* #31	111	Right Hand Independence 3:2 *Son Clave Cáscara* pattern
86			
87	Chords in *Clave* 3:2 *Rumba Clave* #32	112	
88		113	Single Note *Cáscara* Patterns starting from the root 2:3 Son Clave C or C6
89	Implying the *Clave* Advanced 2:3 *Son Clave* #33		
		114	
90		115	Single Note *Cáscara* Patterns 3:2 *Son Clave* C or C6
91	Implying the *Clave* Advanced 3:2 *Son Clave* #34		
		116	
92		117	Single Note *Cáscara* Patterns 2:3 *Son Clave* Cmin or Cmin6
		118	

119	Single Note *Cáscara* Patterns 3:2 *Son Clave* Cmin or Cmin6	145	Single Note *Cáscara* Patterns 2:3 *Son Clave* Cmin7♭5
120		146	
121	Single Note *Cáscara* Patterns 2:3 *Son Clave* Cdim	147	Single Note *Cáscara* Patterns 3:2 *Son Clave* Cmin7♭5
122		148	
123	Single Note *Cáscara* Patterns 3:2 *Son Clave* Cdim	149	Single Note *Cáscara* Patterns 2:3 *Son Clave* Cdim7
124		150	
125	Single Note *Cáscara* Patterns 2:3 *Son Clave* Csus4	151	Single Note *Cáscara* Patterns 3:2 *Son Clave* Cdim7
126		152	
127	Single Note *Cáscara* Patterns 3:2 *Son Clave* Csus4	153	Single Note *Cáscara* Patterns 2:3 *Son Clave* C6
128		154	
129	Single Note *Cáscara* Patterns 2:3 *Son Clave* Caug	155	Single Note *Cáscara* Patterns 3:2 *Son Clave* C6
130		156	
131	Single Note *Cáscara* Patterns 3:2 *Son Clave* Caug	157	Single Note *Cáscara* Patterns 2:3 *Son Clave* Cmin6
132		158	
133	Single Note *Cáscara* Patterns 2:3 *Son Clave* Cmaj7	159	Single Note *Cáscara* Patterns 3:2 *Son Clave* Cmin6
134		160	
135	Single Note *Cáscara* Patterns 3:2 *Son Clave* Cmaj7	161	Single Note *Cáscara* Patterns 2:3 *Son Clave* C7sus4
136		162	
137	Single Note *Cáscara* Patterns 2:3 *Son Clave* C7	163	Single Note *Cáscara* Patterns 3:2 *Son Clave* C7sus4
138		164	
139	Single Note *Cáscara* Patterns 3:2 *Son Clave* C7	165	Single Note *Cáscara* Patterns 2:3 *Son Clave* C7♭5
140		166	
141	Single Note *Cáscara* Patterns 2:3 *Son Clave* Cmin7	167	Single Note *Cáscara* Patterns 3:2 *Son Clave* C7♭5
142		168	
143	Single Note *Cáscara* Patterns 3:2 *Son Clave* Cmin7	169	Single Note *Cáscara* Patterns 2:3 *Son Clave* C7♯5
144		170	

171	Single Note *Cáscara* Patterns 3:2 *Son Clave* C7#5	197	Single Note *Cáscara* Patterns 2:3 *Son Clave* Cmaj7#11 add9
172		198	
173	Single Note *Cáscara* Patterns 2:3 *Son Clave* Cmaj7#11	199	Single Note *Cáscara* Patterns 3:2 *Son Clave* Cmaj7#11 add9
174		200	
175	Single Note *Cáscara* Patterns 3:2 *Son Clave* Cmaj7#11	201	Single Note *Cáscara* Patterns 2:3 *Son Clave* Cmin7add9
176		202	
177	Single Note *Cáscara* Patterns 2:3 *Son Clave* Cmaj7#5	203	Single Note *Cáscara* Patterns 3:2 *Son Clave* Cmin7 add9
178		204	
179	Single Note *Cáscara* Patterns 3:2 *Son Clave* Cmaj7#5	205	Single Note *Cáscara* Patterns 2:3 *Son Clave* Cmin7 add11
180		206	
181	Single Note *Cáscara* Patterns 2:3 *Son Clave* Cmaj7add9	207	Single Note *Cáscara* Patterns 3:2 *Son Clave* Cmin7 add11
182		208	
183	Single Note *Cáscara* Patterns 3:2 *Son Clave* Cmaj7add9	209	Single Note *Cáscara* Patterns 2:3 *Son Clave* Cmin7 add9 variation
184		210	
185	Single Note *Cáscara* Patterns 2:3 *Son Clave* Cmaj7#11 variation	211	Single Note *Cáscara* Patterns 3:2 *Son Clave* Cmin7 add9 variation
186		212	
187	Single Note *Cáscara* Patterns 3:2 *Son Clave* Cmaj7#11 variation	213	Single Note *Cáscara* Patterns 2:3 *Son Clave* C7 add9
188		214	
189	Single Note *Cáscara* Patterns 2:3 *Son Clave* Cmaj7#5 add9	215	Single Note *Cáscara* Patterns 3:2 *Son Clave* C7 add9
190		216	
191	Single Note *Cáscara* Patterns 3:2 *Son Clave* Cmaj7#5 add9	217	Single Note *Cáscara* Patterns 2:3 *Son Clave* Cmaj7 starting from the 3rd
192		218	
193	Single Note *Cáscara* Patterns 2:3 *Son Clave* Cmaj7#5 add9 variation	219	Single Note *Cáscara* Patterns 3:2 *Son Clave* Cm7 starting from the 3rd
194		220	
195	Single Note *Cáscara* Patterns 3:2 *Son Clave* Cmaj7#5 add9 variation	221	Single Note *Cáscara* Patterns 2:3 *Son Clave* Cm7♭5 starting from the 3rd
196		222	

223	Single Note *Cáscara* Patterns 3:2 *Son Clave* Cm7♯5 starting from the 3rd	251	Chords and *Tumbao* with variations #3
224		252	
225	Single Note *Cáscara* Patterns 2:3 *Son Clave* C7 starting from the 5th	253	Chords and *Tumbao* with variations #4
226		254	
227	Single Note *Cáscara* Patterns 3:2 *Son Clave* C7 starting from the 5th	255	Chords and *Tumbao* with variations #5
228		256	
229	Single Note *Cáscara* Pattern 2:3 *Son Clave* C7♭5 starting from the 5th	257	Chords and *Tumbao* with variations #6
230		258	
231	Single Note *Cáscara* Patterns 3:2 *Son Clave* C7♯5 starting from the 5th	259	Chords and *Tumbao* with variations #7
232		260	
233	Single Note *Cáscara* Patterns 2:3 *Son Clave* Cmin7 from the flat7th	261	*Tumbao* in Tenths #8
234		262	
235	Single Note *Cáscara* Patterns 3:2 *Son Clave* Cmin7 from the flat7th	263	2:3 *Son Clave* #1
236		264	
237	Single Note *Cáscara* Patterns 2:3 *Son Clave* C7 from the flat7th	265	3:2 *Son Clave* #2
238		266	
239	Single Note *Cáscara* Patterns 3:2 *Son Clave* C7 from the flat7th	267	*Guajeos/Montunos* one bar phrase #1 2:3 *Son Clave*
240		268	
241	Feeling the subdivision. *Tumbao*	269	*Guajeos/Montunos* one bar phrase #1 3:2 *Son Clave*
242		270	
243	*Tumbao* one bar on and off #1	271	*Guajeos/Montunos* one bar phrase #2 2:3 *Son Clave*
244		272	
245	*Tumbao* one bar on and off #2	273	*Guajeos/Montunos* one bar phrase #2 3:2 *Son Clave*
246		274	
247	Chords and *Tumbao* with variations #1	275	*Cáscara* rhythmic exercise #1 C or C6 2:3 *Son Clave*
248		276	
249	Chords and *Tumbao* with variations #2	277	*Guajeo* Conversion #1 C or C6 2:3 *Son Clave*
250		278	
		279	*Cáscara* rhythmic exercise #2 C or C6 3:2 *Son Clave*
		280	

281	*Guajeo* Conversion (two versions) #1 C or C6 3:2 *Son Clave*	311	Chordal *Montuno* with Inversion of triad (Drop-two to Drop-three voicings)
282		312	
283	*Guajeo* Conversion (two versions) #2 C or C6 3:2 *Son Clave*	313	Yomo Toro "La Pepita de Mango" Guitar Adaptation
284		314	
285	"Adelante" Modern *Guajeo* application	315	Typical *Montuno* in the style of Gilberto "El Pulpo" Colón Jr.
286		316	
287	"Dulcito de Coco" *Guajeo* adaptation	317	*Descarga* Guitar Adaptation of Piano in the style of Bebo Valdés
288		318	
289	"Chucho" *Guajeo* adaptation	319	Typical G Minor vamp
290		320	
291	"Virginiarican Blues"	321	*Montuno* and tenths in *Tumbao* #1
292		322	
293	"Oye mi Tres Montuno" Guitar *Guajeo*	323	*Montuno* and tenths in *Tumbao* #2
294		324	
295	One bar *guajeo* and two bar *guajeo* mix	325	2:3 *Son Clave Guajeo* Octave and Intervals
296		326	
297	Compound and Closed interval *Montuno*	327	2:3 *Son Clave Guajeo* String pairs
298		328	
299	Triadic *Montuno* with Octaves and Intervals Root Position	329	Fmin7 *Guajeo* 2:3 *Son Clave* #1
300		330	
301	Triadic *Montuno* with Octaves and Intervals 1st Inversion	331	Fmin7 *Guajeo* 2:3 *Son Clave* #2
302		332	
303	Triadic *Montuno* with Octaves and Intervals 2nd Inversion	333	Cha-cha-chá 1
304		334	
305	Triadic *Montuno* with Intervals 1st Inversion	335	Cha-cha-chá 2
306		336	
307	Triadic *Montuno* with Intervals 2nd Inversion	337	"Todo Lo que Fuiste" Ex 1
308		338	
309	Triadic *Montuno* with Intervals Root Position	339	"Todo Lo que Fuiste" Ex 2
310		340	
		341	"Todo Lo que Fuiste" Ex 3
		342	

343	"Virginiarican Blues"	349	"Todo lo que fuiste" 2:3 *Rumba Clave* Changes *Montuno* and Improvisation
344		350	
345	Latin Jazz Guitar arrangement of "Bug in a Rug" by Steve Swallow	351	"Cuando tu no estás" Bolero/Cha-cha-chá
346		352	
347	"El Juego" 2:3 *Rumba Clave*	353	"El swing de la finca" *Descarga* 2:3 *Son Clave*
348		354	

Anthology of Influential Guitarists in Latin Jazz

Paul Alicea

Froilán Amezaga

Everett Barksdale

Ahmed Barroso

Jose Lorenzo "Che" Benitez

George Benson

Bob Bianco

Kenny Burrell

Pablo Cano

Jorge Chicoy

Eddie Duran

Danny Embrey

Barry Galbraith

Grant Green

Marcelino Guerra

Sonny Henry

Neff Irizarry II

Barney Kessel

Steve Khan

Jorge Laboy

Benjamin Lapidus

Juanito Márquez

Pablo Menendez

Edgardo Miranda

Wes Montgomery

Carlos Emilio "El Gordo" Morales

Ray Obiedo

David Oquendo

Peruchin Jr.

John Quara

Leo Quintero

Jimmy Raney

Karl Ratzer

Bob Redfield

Ñico Rojas

Jorge Salinas

Frankie Sánchez

Carlos Santana

Jorge Santana

Ito Serrano

Ramón Stagnaro

Rene Toledo

Atilla Zoller

Rick Zunigar

Richie Zellón

Timeline of Selected Recordings

1950–present	Juanito Márquez y su combo
1950s–	Omara Portuondo featuring Juanito Márquez
1950s–	Froilán Amézaga with Elena Burke
1950s–	*Una noche con Felipe Dulzaides y su cuarteto* featuring Pablo Cano
1955–77	Pablo Paul "Payo" Alicea and Frankie "Pancho" Sánchez, La Playa Sextet. Later, Frankie Sánchez would form the rival group, La Plata Sextette.
1957–	Tito Puente RCA recordings, *Night Beat* and *Mucho Puente*
	John Quara, "Son de la Loma" with piano
	Barry Galbraith played on *Mambo Beat*, *Malibu Beat* and *Night Ritual*
	(Played on Chico O'Farrill record) *Mambo Beat*
	Francisco Sánchez (La Playa Sextet)
1960–	Pablo Cano with Roberto Ledesma, *Guitarra Bohémia*
1960–	Los Admiradores, *Bongos, Flutes and Guitars* featuring Tony Mottola.
1961–	Barney Kessel, *Contemporary Latin Rhythms* on Reprise Records. This would be the first Latin Jazz recording with guitar as the featured main melodic instrument.
1962–	Grant Green's *The Latin Bit*. This would be the second Latin Jazz outing for a jazz guitarist, but there is an absence of the traditional Latin jazz percussion, and Grant fulfills more of the "jazz" bit while the repertoire fits the "Latin" bit. His soloing is confined to jazz swing with no attempt at accentuating the *clave*.
1962–69–	José Lorenzo "Che" Benítez with Peregoyo y su Combo Vacaná.
1964–	Kenny Burrell on "Afro Blue" from Cal Tjader's *Soul Sauce*.
1964–	Attila Zoller on "Mambo Dinero" on Dave Pike's *Manhattan Latin*.
1964–	Jimmy Raney on Cal Tjader's "Leyte" from *Breeze from the East*.

1966–	Attila Zoller on "Manteca" from Cal Tjader's *Soul Burst*.
1966–	Barry Galbraith and Everett Barksdale on Clarke Terry and Chico O'Farrill's "Spanish Rice."
1967–	Sonny Henry on Willie Bobo's "Juicy," "Bobo Motion," "Spanish Blues Band,""A New Dimension,""Spanish Grease"and "1 2 y 3" (Verve).
1967–	Sonny Henry on Chico O'Farrill's *Married Well* (Verve).
1969–	Bob Bianco on "My Spiritual Indian" from Eddie Palmieri's *Justicia* (Tico Records).
1973–2009	Edgardo Miranda with Cortijo and his Time Machine, Tito Puente, Jerry Gonzalez and Daniel Ponce, among others.
1974–2001	Carlos Emilio Morales with Grupo Irakere. Carlos mixes jazz, funk and rock guitar elements with Afro-Cuban.
1974–	Jorge Santana featured on "Ratón" with *Fania All Stars Live in Africa*.
1976–	George Benson played on "Old Devil Moon"(a Sonny Bravo arrangement) from *BENSON/FARRELL*.
1977–	Eric Gale and John Tropea on Fania All-Stars' *Rhythm Machine*.
1977–	Bob Redfield with Cal Tjader on "Cuban Fantasy," "Puttin' it Together" and "Here."
1978–	Karl Ratzer on Ray Mantilla's *Mantilla* (Inner City).
1978–	Ito Serrano on Roberto Roena y su Apollo Sounds *El Progreso*
1979–	Ito Serrano on Salsa Fever Orchestra's "Que vivan los estudiantes."
1980–1981	Guitarists with Clare Fischer: Danny Embrey on "Crazy Bird" and "Salsa Picante," and Rick Zunigar on "Machaca."
1980–	René Toledo with Grupo Afrocuba.
1983–	George Benson on "My Latin Brother" from Jorge Dalto & Super Friends' *Rendez-Vous* (Eastworld).

1974–2019	Steve Khan, "Tightrope" 1977 "The Blue Man" 1978 "Arrows" 1979 "Eyewitness" 1983 "Casa Loco" 1990 "Public Access" 1994 "Crossings" 1999 "The Green Field" 2005 "Borrowed Time" 2007 "Parting Shot" 2011 "Subtext" 2014 "Backlog" 2016 "Patchwork" 2019
1993–	Bobby Sanabria, *New York City Aché* featuring Edgardo Miranda
1996–	Peruchin Jr. & the Cuban All Stars, *Descarga Dos*
1999–2000	Caribbean Latin Jazz Project featuring Steve Khan, *New Horizons* and *Paraíso*
2001	Neff Irizarry, *Nepenthe*
2004	Bebo Valdés, *Bebo de Cuba* featuring Edgardo Miranda
2016	Ray Obiedo, *Latin Jazz Project Vol. 1*

Credits

Transcriptions	Neff Irizarry II
Layout and Design	Ian Carey
Proofreading	Victor Mendoza, Randy Vincent, and Rebeca Mauleón
Photographs	Roberts Vidzidskis
Recording	Neff Irizarry II Guitars
Bass	Leslie Lopez
Percussion	Ricardo Padilla
Mixing and Mastering	Aleksandr Wolk and Neff Irizarry II Wolk Recording Studios, Riga, Latvia
Guitars	Gibson ES-175D and Gibson ES-345 Custom Shop Mono
Amplifier	Pearce G2r and Mesa Boogie 1x12 open back cabinets

About the Author

A highly talented composer and guitarist specializing in Latin and contemporary jazz, **Neff Irizarry** follows in the footsteps of Jim Hall, Pat Metheny, and Steve Khan. His unique blend of progressive Latin jazz is a display of Puerto Rican "sabor" and a Nordic cool called "Sisu."

Featured in *The European Real Book* (Sher Music Co., 2007), Neff has joined the ranks of the most esteemed European composers of jazz.

His critically acclaimed debut CD *Nepenthe* in 2000, which was produced by Grammy Award-winning bassist Jimmy Haslip, features the guitar in a Latin jazz context without the piano.

Neff's creativity, dedication, and solid groove as a guitarist have also enabled him to perform with Eddie Henderson, Jimmy Haslip, Lonnie Liston Smith, Victor Mendoza, Brian Melvin, Anders Bergcrantz and Deniss Pashkevich, among others at numerous international clubs and festivals.

A B.M. and M.M. graduate from the Berklee College of Music, Neff believes in the power of education and self-development. As a result, Neff has been an in-demand educator with over twenty years of experience in Northern Europe as a teacher and clinician.

> "Neff Irizarry has embarked down a path traveled by few guitarists in contemporary jazz and certainly contemporary Latin jazz! To execute all the *montunos, guajeos*, necessary harmonizations, and to solo with clarity and fire is a tall order but Neff is certainly up to the task."
>
> —**Steve Khan**, guitarist
> The Voice of Latin Jazz Guitar

Sher Music Co.
The World's Premier Jazz & Latin Publisher!

BEST-SELLING BOOKS BY MARK LEVINE
- The Jazz Theory Book
- The Jazz Piano Book
- Jazz Piano Masterclass: The Drop 2 Book
- How to Voice Standards at the Piano

THE WORLD'S BEST FAKE BOOKS
- The New Real Book - Vol. 1 - C, Bb and Eb
- The New Real Book - Vol. 2 - C, Bb and Eb
- The New Real Book - Vol. 3 - C, Bb and Eb
- The Real Easy Book - Vol. 1 - C, Bb, Eb and Bass Clef (Three-Horn Edition)
- The Real Easy Book - Vol. 2 - C, Bb, Eb and Bass Clef
- The Real Easy Book - Vol. 3 - C, Bb, Eb and Bass Clef
- The Latin Real Easy Book - C, Bb, Eb and Bass Clef
- The Standards Real Book - C, Bb and Eb
- The Latin Real Book - C, Bb and Eb
- The Real Cool Book - West Coast 'Cool' Jazz Octet Charts
- The All-Jazz Real Book - C, Bb and Eb
- The European Real Book - C, Bb and Eb
- The Best of Sher Music Real Books - C, Bb and Eb
- The World's Greatest Fake Book - C version only
- The Yellowjackets Songbook - (all parts)

DIGITAL FAKE BOOKS (at shermusic.com only)
- The New Real Book - Vol.1 - C, Bb and Eb
- The Digital Standards Songbook
- The Digital Real Book
- The Jazz Songbook Series

LATIN MUSIC BOOKS
- **Decoding Afro-Cuban Jazz: The Music of Chucho Valdés and Irakere** - by Chucho Valdés and Rebeca Mauleón
- The Salsa Guidebook - by Rebeca Mauleón
- The Latin Real Easy Book - C, Bb, Eb and Bass Clef
- The Latin Bass Book - by Oscar Stagnaro and Chuck Sher
- The True Cuban Bass - by Carlos del Puerto and Silvio Vergara
- The Brazilian Guitar Book - by Nelson Faria
- Inside the Brazilian Rhythm Section - by Nelon Faria/Cliff Korman
- The Conga Drummer's Guidebook - by Michael Spiro
- Language of the Masters - by Michael Spiro
- Introduction to the Conga Drum, DVD - by Michael Spiro
- Afro-Caribbean Grooves for Drumset - by Jean-Philippe Fanfant
- Afro-Peruvian Percussion Ensemble - by Hector Morales
- Flamenco Improvisation, Vol. 1-3 - by Enrique Vargas

Bilingual or Libros en Español
- The Latin Real Book - C, Bb and Eb
- 101 Montunos - by Rebeca Mauleón
- Muy Caliente! - Afro-Cuban Book Play-Along CD
- El Libro del Jazz Piano - by Mark Levine
- Teoria del Jazz - by Mark Levine (digital only)

ALL METHOD BOOKS ALSO AVAILABLE IN DIGITAL FORM ONLINE

JAZZ METHOD BOOKS

BASS
- The Improvisor's Bass Method - by Chuck Sher
- Concepts for Bass Soloing - by Marc Johnson & Chuck Sher
- Walking Bassics - by Ed Fuqua
- Foundation Exercises for Bass - by Chuck Sher

GUITAR
- Jazz Guitar Voicings: The Drop 2 Book - by Randy Vincent
- Three-Note Voicings and Beyond - by Randy Vincent
- Line Games - by Randy Vincent
- Jazz Guitar Soloing: The Cellular Approach - by Randy Vincent
- The Guitarist's Introduction to Jazz - by Randy Vincent

PIANO
- Playing for Singers - by Mike Greensill
- An Approach to Comping: The Essentials - by Jeb Patton
- An Approach to Comping, Vol.2: Advanced - by Jeb Patton
- Wisdom of the Hand - by Marius Nordal
- Intro to Jazz Piano, A Deep Dive - by Jeb Patton

OTHER INSTRUMENTS
- Inner Drumming - by George Marsh
- Method for Chromatic Harmonica - by Max de Aloe
- Modern Etudes for Solo Trumpet - by Cameron Pearce
- New Orleans Trumpet - by Jim Thornton

FOR ALL INSTRUMENTS
- The Jazz Harmony Book - by David Berkman
- Jazz Musician's Guide to Creative Practicing - by D. Berkman
- The Jazz Singers Guide Book - by David Berkman
- Metaphors for the Musician - by Randy Halberstadt
- Forward Motion - by Hal Galper
- The Serious Jazz Practice Book - by Barry Finnerty
- The Serious Jazz Book II - by Barry Finnerty
- Building Solo Lines From Cells - by Randy Vincent
- The Real Easy Ear Training Book - by Roberta Radley
- Reading, Writing and Rhythmetic - by Roberta Radley
- Minor is Major - by Dan Greenblatt
- Jazz Scores and Analysis - Vol. 1 - by Rick Lawn
- Essential Grooves - by Moretti, Nicholl and Stagnaro
- The Jazz Solos of Chick Corea - transcribed by Peter Sprague

FOR STUDENT MUSICIANS
- The Blues Scales - by Dan Greenblatt - C, Bb and Eb
- Rhythm First! - by Tom Kamp - C, Bb, Eb and Bass Clef
- The Guitarist's Introduction to Jazz - Randy Vincent
- Jazz Songs for Student Violinists - by Keefe and Mitchell

CDs
- Poetry+Jazz: A Magical Marriage
- The New Real Book Play-Along CDs (for Vol.1) - #1, 2 and 3
- The Latin Real Book Sampler CD
- The Music of Charles Stevens

For more info, see SherMusic.com